Wilmette: a history

George D. Bushnell

D1500494

Editor: Ben Kartman
Graphics/Layout/Cover Design: Joanne Andrews
Production Supervision: John P. Ryan

The Wilmette Bicentennial Commission
Wilmette, Illinois

The antique woodcut used on the cover and
on chapter title pages is taken from the official
Village seal, chosen by Charles Boggs and
Alexander McDaniel in 1872.

Photographs and documents, unless otherwise credited,
are from the collections of the Wilmette Historical
Museum and Wilmette Public Library.

Contents

FOREWORD

It is often rewarding to take the dictionary from the shelf and look up the key word of the subject at hand — in this case, History. Webster tells us that "History is an account of what has happened in the life or development of a people, country, institution, etc. A systematic account that is usually in chronological order with an analysis and explanation." The definition ends with " Make History . . . . to do or be something important enough to be recorded."

The story these pages have to tell, more than fulfill these precise specifications. Although the area described is not the usual vast panorama, in fact only a scant 5.3 square miles (correction: 13.7 square kilometers) it is nevertheless a complete and warmly nostalgic portrait of a tiny segment of the world that came to be known as Wilmette, Illinois, U.S.A.

The dedicated men and women who serve on the 1976 Bicentennial Commission have unanimously agreed that here was "something important enough to be recorded." We have them to thank for conceiving and producing this work not only as the collected treasures of the past, but also, and most importantly, as a gift to the future. In that regard, it is interesting to note that the paper on which this chronicle is printed will, according to the best estimate of the manufacturer, last for at least three hundred years . . . presuming that the reader and his descendants treat the volume with reasonable care and a measure of respect.

Let's see, three hundred years from now would be the year 2276, time for another "centennial celebration." Surely then, if the nation and the municipality continue to exist and if this or one of its sister volumes fulfills its life expectancy, there will be in existence a prize item of antiquity worthy of display and study at that inevitable Quinque-Centennial.

One cannot help but speculate on how those future people, some fifteen generations hence, will think of us present day Wilmettians, based on what they read and see among the then stiff and faded pages. Will they regard us and our founders as somewhat barbaric, blindly ignorant in our stumbling twentieth century conventions? Possibly, on the other hand, we may be remembered as the happy children of a golden age, fortunate to have lived in a time of unduplicated independence and freedom.

What they might not grasp so readily is the formation of a late twentieth century social institution. How, starting with the geological dawn down through eons of glaciers and virgin forest a prosperous community was destined to emerge here. With this book as a guide they, as well as the contemporary reader, will see unfolding from these chapters an evolving social tapestry woven in rich detail of the year to year and day to day development which has given this place its unique character. Why, starting with the first family to build a cabin home on the shores of Lake Michigan, the area has continued to attract citizens of talent, character, and leadership whose willingness to serve has enhanced the natural attributes.

A community, most simply stated, is "a group of people living together in the same place under the same laws." By that standard alone a review of our heritage will reveal that Wilmette is and has been a successful village. From the earliest Potawatomi camps to the newest arriving families, there is a common bond — a universal quest that for so many is fulfilled here . . . . it is a desirable place to live one's life, to work, to raise a family . . . . let us fervently hope that it will remain so for all time.

Warren L. Burmeister
31st President of the
Village of Wilmette

July, 1976

PREFACE

Wilmette: A History owes its existence to a dedicated group of Village residents, past and present, whose concern for preserving community history has made the book possible. Pioneer families who arrived in the 1870's, 1880's and 1890's, many of them members of Ye Olde Towne Folkes, and others who came here in later years preserved and shared records, recollections and photographs, which have been the basis for this history.

From the very first planning discussions early in the winter of 1975 it was agreed that this book should include a generous helping of photographs, maps and drawings, together with personal recollections, to bring back times long past more vividly for our readers. Text and illustrations have been combined by chapter periods, to tell the Village story chronologically from the beginning through the first half of 1976.

To all those who have so generously contributed to make this book possible, and to those who will continue to cherish and preserve our local history, this book is gratefully dedicated. If Antoine and Archange Ouilmette could see how their lakeside cabin in the forest wilderness has become a lovely community, we think they would be pleased and proud, too.

George D. Bushnell

Wilmette, Illinois
July, 1976

ACKNOWLEDGEMENTS

Many people have helped in the writing of this book, and their interest in preserving and in sharing Village history deserves the recognition and appreciation of the entire community. One person in particular has been an inspired talent and source of historical knowledge throughout the project. Working with her husband, Dave, Joanne Andrews is responsible not only for the outstanding typography and book layout completed under a very tight time schedule, but also for valuable suggestions and additions of material, based on her broad knowledge of Wilmette's history. These contributions have materially improved and brightened the book, and the author acknowledges his very great debt to her.

James A. Williams has devoted years of time and energy to the collecting and organization of historical materials as a leader in the Wilmette Historical Commission and Society, and has made the job of researching the book far easier.

Ben Kartman has lent his many years of experience in editing and writing to edit the manusacript, and his suggestions and corrections have been invaluable.

The book has been produced with funds granted by the Board of Trustees, and became a reality only because of their considerable faith in the project. A non-profit venture, money from sales of the book will be used to reimburse the Village for the grant. Pre-sale promotion of the book has been directed by Charles E. Hayes, Jr., whose promotion and marketing expertise has been essential to the project.

A special note of thanks is due Wilmette teenager Christine Bohlman, who spent many hours carefully indexing the book, bringing to her work a professionalism far beyond her age. And for their encouragement and understanding, I affectionately thank my wife, Faith, and our children George, Christie, Elizabeth and Stuart.

Finally, a word of appreciation to the following, for their contributions of information and photographs: Bill and Jane Alexander, Mrs. John Cossarek of the Woman's Club of Wilmette, George Campbell, William Robertson, Rhea Adler, Matilda M. Kempe, George Fred Keck, David Randle, Gordon Wallace, Mrs. Florence Doherty, Mrs. William Henrich, Dave Leach, Jr., Henry Hoffman, Kay Schultz, Joanne Prim Shade, Fred Egloff, L. Roy Wilcox, Lea Bohlman, Mrs. James Crabb, Charles Jules Michelet, Jr., and Dick Thompson and the Wilmette Public Library staff. We appreciate the assistance of Rand McNally & Company in procuring paper for the book.

George D. Bushnell

Wilmette, Illinois

July, 1976

1
Prehistoric Days to Pottawatomies

North America in the Great Ice Age. The shaded area shows the maximum ice sheet. Arrows indicate the direction of flow. Approximately 50,000 B.C.

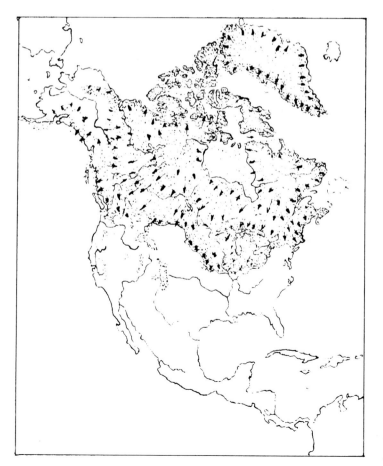

Glacial moraines as left around the end of Lake Michigan. Shown shaded. Drawings by Charles C. Henderson, 1949.

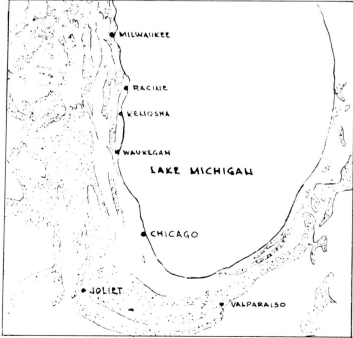

Indian Mound-Builder Artifact, Excavated in July, 1922. The fired clay model of a head was discovered in a sand ridge from three to five feet deep, when a laborer was excavating a trench for a water pipe, in the rear of J. Melville Brown's home at 738 Eleventh Street July 10, 1922. Evidently broken from a larger object, possibly a bowl or water vessel, the artifact is thought to date to the mound-builder culture, perhaps 600-800 years ago.

At first, the entire central valley area of North America was covered by a great sea teeming with strange marine animals. When the ocean finally receded after millions of years, the land which includes Wilmette was a swamp, in habited by reptiles and huge flying insects, and covered with steamy forests of trees and plants. Then the land grew colder, and huge glaciers moved slowly down from the north, grinding the land flat and depositing rocks and boulders. Underneath the land was a great expanse of bedrock, formed under pressure from millions of fossil animals and sediment from the sea, and hardened during eons of time.

More than 12,000 years ago, the last glacial ice field melted, forming Lake Chicago, the larger ancestor of Lake Michigan. The glaciers left scattered, rounded mounds of debris called moraines on the flat expanse of prairieland. They also trapped small pockets of water; some flowed west to the Mississippi River and some filled the cracks through the moraines to form the Calumet Sag Channel. The melting glacial ice sheet also formed sandy strips which remained high and dry above the marshy land.

Lake Michigan, as we know it today, was at a much higher level, reaching west to our present Ridge Road. For thousands of years, the lake currents carried material eroded from lakeside cliffs to the north, and deposited the debris as a submerged bar of gravel and sand. As the water receded, the bar appeared above water as a bay, reaching from Winnetka to Rose Hill in Chicago. The bay became a marsh and one of the ridges of beach became the Green Bay Trail.

4

For several thousand years, the North Shore was a land of thick woods, inhabited by Indian tribes which traveled the lake shoreline and built great earthen mounds to bury their dead. In July, 1922, a laborer digging a trench for a water pipe back of J. Melville Brown's lot on Eleventh Street unearthed a small clay model of a human head, broken off from another object. The clay head was examined and identified as part of an Indian Moundbuilder's effigy bowl. Although no one knows how it came to that spot, it is one bit of

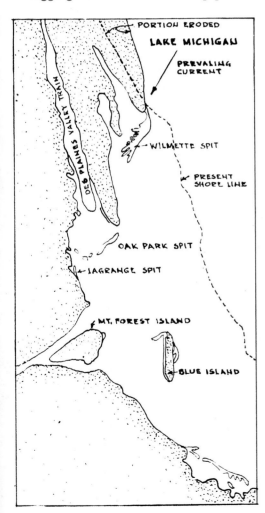

Glenwood Stage

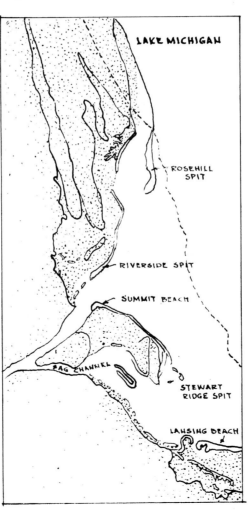

Calumet Stage

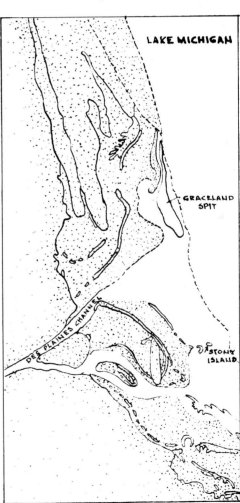

Toleston Stage.

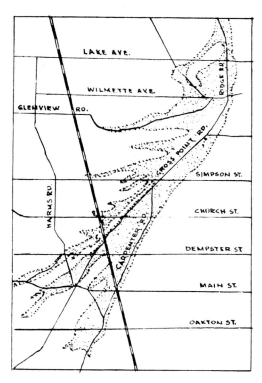

Lake Chicago's changes that developed the Wilmette area. Sketch map of "Wilmette Spit" enlarged from that shown on p. 3. Note how the Indian trails followed the high ground of the "Spit."

How "Lake Chicago" was filled in to give us the shore line of our Lake Michigan. Showing the several stages wherein, due to the prevailing North East/South West lake current, the spoil from the wave action on the North Shore bluffs was gradually deposited to the South, making Chicago's land.

proof that prehistoric Indians lived or traveled here. Many centuries later, the Pottawatomies established a village near the lake, attracted by the ease of water travel, abundant game and thick woods.

And there is evidence that an expedition of black-robed Jesuit priests, led by Saint Cosme, beached their canoes at some point near the Grosse Pointe headland on October 20, 1698, driven ashore by a sudden squall of wind. The party of priests had come from Michillimackinac in northern Michigan, heading for the Mississippi by way of Wisconsin and portage to the Fox River. But because the rivers were low and the portage would be too long, they changed their route and paddled towards Chicago, until the wind forced them to land, after throwing much of their cargo into the lake.

Almost a century later, Jean Baptiste Point du Sable established a trading post at the mouth of the Chicago River, returning after the Revolutionary War to build Chicago's first permanent house, a twenty-two by forty foot log cabin which he left in 1800.

Ten years earlier, in 1790, a 30-year old French Canadian employee of the American Fur Company named Antoine Ouilmette had arrived at the site of an Indian settlement called Checaugau, from his home at Lahndrayh, near Montreal. As a traveling trader for the company, Ouilmette visited the Indian settlements and met Archange Chevallier, daughter of Francois Chevallier, a French trader, and his part-Indian wife. They were married in 1796 or 1797, legend says, in the woods of Grosse Pointe, near several Pottawatomie villages. Archange was born at Sugar Creek, Michigan, in 1764. The Ouilmette's had eight children, four sons

Racine June 1th 1839

Mr John Kinzie

Sir my home affairs are sutch that I cannot leave to see you at present. I caim into Chicago in The year 1790 in July, witness old Mr Veaux he knows i was theare and Mr Greano and Mr provaunsell and Shappee and Mr law and F. Bullbonea These men weare liveing in the Country Before the war with the winnebagoes Trading with them I Saw the indians Brake open the Door of my house. and also the Door of Mr Kinzies house at first theare was onely three indians Come they told me there was Forty more comeing and they told me To run i Did So, in nine days all i found left of my things The feathers of my Beds Scattered about the floor, the amount Distroyed By them at that time was about Eight hundred Dollars Besides your fathar and me Had about four hundred hogs Distroyd By the Saim indians and nearly at the Saim time further Particulars when i See you I wish you to nite me whether it is Best for me to Come thare Ar for you to Come hear and how Soon it must Be Done

yours with Respect
Wm Moore   Antoine his X Ouilmell mark

(WAFER)

Antoine Ouilmette arrives in Chicago. Signed with his "x" mark, Ouilmette wrote a letter dated June 1, 1839, to his old friend John H. Kinzie, giving details of his early life in the tiny settlement of Chicago. The letter was written in Racine, where he owned a farmstead.

and four daughters: Joseph, Louis, Francis, Mitchell, Elizabeth, Archange, Josette and Sophia, as well as an adopted daughter, Archange Trombla.

Many years later, Ouilmette prepared a letter at Racine, Wisconsin, dated June 1, 1839, addressed to John H. Kinzie and signed with "his X mark":

"My home affairs are sutch that I cannot leave to see you at present.

"I caim into Chicago in the year 1790 in July witness old Mr. Veaux. . .and Mr. Griano. . . These men were living in the country Before the war with the winnebagoes. Trading with them I saw the Indians Brake open the Door of my house and also the Door of Mr. Kinzie's House. At first there was only three Indians come. They told me there was Forty more coming and they told me to run. I did So. In nine days all I found left of my things was the feathers of my beds scattered about the floor, the amount Destroyed by them at that time was about Eight hundred Dollars. Besides your father and me Had about four hundred hogs Destroyed by the Saim Indians and nearly at the Saim time. further particulars when I See you. I wish you to write me whether it is best for me come thare or for you to come here and how soon it must be Done"

Archange Ouilmette.
Daughter of a French trader, the Pottawatomie Indian woman married Antoine in 1796 or 1797, and by the Treaty of Prairie du Chien in 1829, was granted two sections of 1,280 acres comprising the present sites of Wilmette and north Evanston. Painting is artist George Lusk's conception — no portrait from life is known to exist.

Schoolcraft's View of Chicago, 1820. Drawing included "every house in the village," and was made from a flat sand area, according to Henry Schoolcraft. Author of extensive geological and geographical studies of the midwest, the pioneer American ethnologist (1793-1864) surveyed the Great Lakes in the 1820's, later pioneering studies of the Indian tribes.

In 1803, Ouilmette owned one of the four cabins which comprised the tiny Chicago settlement. Nearly a century later, a grandson, I. J. Martell, recalled that his mother, Sophia Martell, talked about her father's early days, when he furnished Fort Dearborn with beef, pork and cordwood, and traveled between the settlement and a farm he owned at Racine, Wisconsin, as well as to Milwaukee and Canada.

In August, 1812, Ouilmette and his family were responsible for saving two lives during the old Fort Dearborn massacre by the Pottawatomies. Fort Dearborn had been built in 1803 and named after General Henry Dearborn. When the War of 1812 began, the fort was commanded by Captain Nathan Heald. Heald was ordered to leave the fort and move his troops and the settlers to the safer Detroit area. Although his troops in the fort urged their commander not to leave the fort because of the danger of an Indian attack, Heald decided to obey orders and on August 15, 1812, marched out of the fort with 67 soldiers and 30 settlers. But when the party had reached what is now 18th Street near Lake Michigan, a band of 500 Pottawatomies and their allies attacked the small force, and killed half the group, returning the next day to burn Fort Dearborn.

In her book, *Wau-bun*, Mrs. John H. Kinzie described that terrible event, the day following the massacre of the Fort's inhabitants. A band of Pottawatomies arrived at the site. Angry because they had missed the massacre and plunder, they were ready to take revenge on the few survivors, including Mrs. Helm, wife of an officer, and other members of the Kinzie family. Black Partridge, the Pottawatomie chief who had saved the life of Mrs. Helm, told her to dress as a Frenchwoman, and took her to Ouilmette's house, where she was hidden under a large feather bed. Despite the heat of the day, Archange Ouilmette's sister, Mrs. Bisson, sat on the bed with her sewing. When the Indians entered to search the house, she sat calmly working on a quilt, until the war party left. Just as the Indians left, a noncommissioned officer named Griffin, who had escaped the massacre and hidden in the currant bushes in Ouilmette's garden, climbed into the house through a window. The Ouilmette family quickly stripped him of his uniform and gave him a deerskin suit, with belt, moccasins and pipe, like a French trader, in which he was able to escape.

So friendly were relations between Ouilmette and the Indians that the Ouilmette family stayed on in the cabin after the Kinzies and the other white settlers had fled. Ouilmette was very likely the only white settler of Chicago for the next four years. In 1814, Alexander Robinson, later chief of the Pottawatomies, came to the tiny settlement and with Ouilmette grew corn in the Fort's former garden. In 1816, when the Fort was rebuilt, they sold the crop to Captain Bradley. Thrifty and ambitious, Ouilmette built up a herd of oxen, horses and cattle, operated a small store, continued his trade with the Indians, and sold the wool from his sheep to make yarn for stockings for the soldiers.

According to a Chicago tax roll dated July 25, 1825, Ouilmette paid $4.00 in taxes on property valued at $400.00, and the following year was listed as a voter in an election on August 7, casting his vote for John Quincy Adams for President.

Shortly after voting for President Adams, Ouilmette and his family moved north and built a cabin on a bluff overlooking the lake, just north of Lake

Kinzie House in Chicago, 1832. Arriving in Chicago in 1804, John Kinzie was a trader and provider for Fort Dearborn. Cottage was on the present site of the Equitable Life building at 401 North Michigan Avenue. (A. T. Andreas, *History of Chicago,* from a description by John H. Kinzie.)

Indian Trails as of 1804. Drawing by Charles C. Henderson, 1949, from Scharf's map of 1900. Mr. Henderson, noted architect and long-time Wilmette resident, did extensive research for his drawings done for the Wilmette Historical Commission, 1949-1956.

Avenue. White settlers were now beginning to move into northern Illinois and southern Wisconsin, and by the summer of 1827, the Indians of the region were restless and angry, resenting the movement of the white man into their lands. On July 29, 1829, the Treaty of Prairie du Chien was concluded, giving the United States title to huge areas of land from Lake Michigan west to the Rock River. The treaty was a starting wedge designed to oust the Indians from Illinois and Wisconsin. Signing the treaty were 30 Indian braves and five squaws., representing the Chippewas, Ottawas and Pottawatomies.

Most important, the treaty also created the original Ouilmette Reservation. Article Four provided for a grant of land to Archange Ouilmette, in recognition of the help of Antoine in persuading the Indians to sign the Treaty:

"To Archange Ouilmette, a Pottawatomie woman, wife of Antoine, two sections for herself and her children on Lake Michigan, south of and adjoining the northern boundary of the cession herein made by the Indians aforesaid to the United States. . . The Tracts of land herein stipulated to be granted shall never be leased or conveyed by the grantees, or their heirs, to any person whatever, without the permission of the President of the United States."

These two sections, 1280 acres, extended from Elmwood Avenue south to Central Street, Evanston, and from the lake west to a line along what is now Fifteenth Street, so that about 300 acres fell within the present boundaries of Evanston. Although no contemporary picture of the Ouilmette cabin exists,

pioneer Wilmette settler Alexander McDaniel remembered being a guest of the family on August 14, 1836: "The house. . . was a large hewed log blockhouse, considered in those days good enough for a congressman to live in. . ." In March, 1908, Charles P. Westerfield, son of the pioneer settler John G. Westerfield, recalled seeing the cabin as a child, in 1857, years after the Ouilmette family left the area. The boy twice watched a small band of Indians leave the Green Bay trail and go up to the cabin as if remembering an earlier era. Also at this time, Charles Westerfield did a water color drawing of the cabin as he remembered it. Within 100 feet of the cabin was a small Indian burial mound, about 15 feet long by four feet high.

In April, 1833, Ouilmette and members of the Mark Beaubien family, who had settled in the area, sent a petition for Chicago's first Catholic church to the Bishop of the Missouri diocese in St. Louis. Staunch Catholics, they urged the bishop that a "priest should be sent there before other sects obtain the upper hand, which very likely they will try to do." The bishop acted very quickly, granting the request for what was to be St. Mary's Church on April 17, only a day after the petition was received.

That same year, Ouilmette received $800 for his services when the Treaty of Chicago was negotiated, a year after the Blackhawk War.

Ouilmette and Archange lived on the Ouilmette Reservation until 1838. According to Frank R. Grover, in his pamphlet "Antoine Ouilmette" (Evanston Historical Society, 1908), Benjamin F. Hill, an early Wilmette settler, said that Mr. Joseph Fountain of Evanston, and others, were prosecuted by Ouilmette

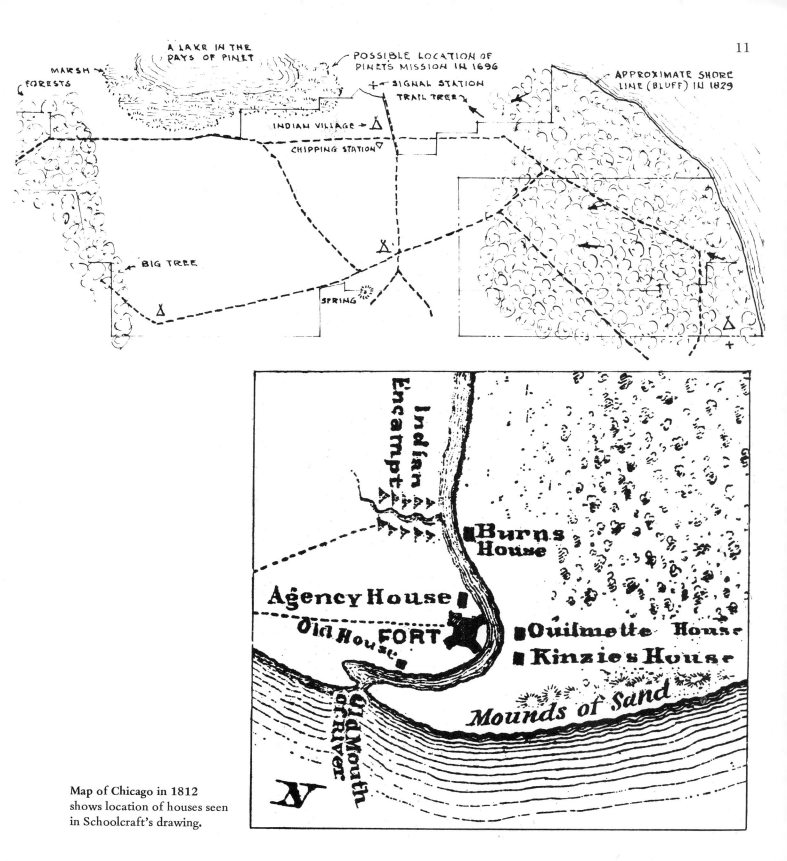

MARSH FORESTS

A LAKE IN THE PAYS OF PINET

POSSIBLE LOCATION OF PINET'S MISSION IN 1696

SIGNAL STATION

TRAIL TREE

INDIAN VILLAGE

CHIPPING STATION

APPROXIMATE SHORE LINE (BLUFF) IN 1829

BIG TREE

SPRING

Indian Encampt.

Burns House

Agency House

Old House FORT

Ouilmette House

Kinzie's House

Old Mouth or River

Mounds of Sand

N

Map of Chicago in 1812
shows location of houses seen
in Schoolcraft's drawing.

John Doyle's log cabin on the lake shore. Built by John Doyle sometime in the 1820's, and pictured here shortly after the turn of the century, the cabin was the site of the wedding of Elizabeth Ouilmette to Michael Welch May 11, 1830. Welch was said to be the first Irish settler in Chicago, and the wedding was reputedly the first on the North Shore.

Pioneer Roads Shown From the Rees Map of 1852. Drawing by Charles C. Henderson, 1949.

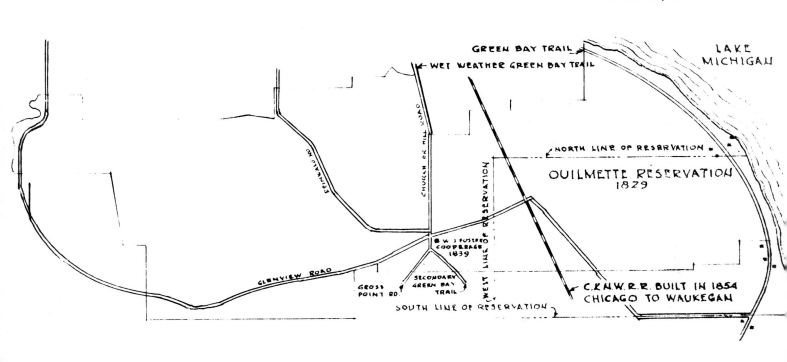

"for trespassing upon the reservation by cutting timber." Ouilmette lost the suit and paid "a large bill of court costs." Fountain's lawyer collected by having the Sheriff confiscate and sell two "fine Indian ponies" belonging to Ouilmette, "which were his special pride." It was immediately after this injustice (Ouilmette very likely did not hire a lawyer) that Ouilmette left the reservation, as Grover observed, "never to return." Both in their late seventies, the Ouilmettes decided to move west with the Pottawatomies across the Mississippi. On November 25, 1840, Archange died at Council Bluffs, Iowa, and Antoine followed her in December, 1841.

By the terms of the Treaty of Prairie du Chien, neither Archange nor her children could sell any of the land granted to them without the consent of the President of the United States. But the land was highly prized because of the thick stand of timber, which was already being cut by outsiders when the Ouilmette family occupied their lakeside cabin. In a petition to the President of the United States dated February 22, 1844, seven of the heirs of Archange Ouilmette (except Joseph who kept his share of the land and sold it later) asked for permission to sell the land, explaining that because they lived so far away the land was declining in value "by having much of its timber, which constitutes its chief worth, cut off and stolen by various individuals living near by." Further more, they said, it was against their "feelings and interests" to live away from their tribe. The petition ended by suggesting that "Your

Antoine and Archange Ouilmette's Cabin. This drawing from memory by Charles P. Westerfield recalls the lakeshore cabin which young Alexander McDaniel found "fit for any congressman," after dining in 1836 with the Ouilmette family. The cabin was located near the lakeshore just north of Lake Avenue, and was occupied from 1828 until 1844.

14

Excellency will cause the Government of the United States to purchase back from us said Reserve of land and pay us one dollar and twenty-five cents per acre therefor." Finally, the Ouilmette children urged action as soon as possible, because they "are now at Chicago on expense, waiting for the termination of this petition, and anxious to return home as soon as possible." In answer to the petition, Henry W. Clarke was appointed as a special agent to sell the land owned by the seven children to real estate speculators for as fair a price as possible, during the years 1844 and 1845. The south half of the Ouilmette Reservation, an area of 640 acres including the entire part in what is now north Evanston, sold for $1,000, or about $1.50 per acre. The north section was sold in smaller parcels for a larger sum. Joseph Ouilmette sold his share of the land separately for $460, using the money to improve his farm in

Marathon County, Wisconsin, where he lived until he, too, went to live at the Pottawatomie Reservation at St. Mary's, Kansas. The sale of the Ouilmette Reservation set the stage for settlement which was to make possible the birth of Wilmette.

IN COMMEMORATION OF ANTOINE OUILMETTE, FIRST WHITE SETTLER, WHO IN 1829 BUILT HIS LOG CABIN NEAR THIS SITE. TO HIS WIFE ARCHANGE OF THE POTTAWATOMIE TRIBE THE FEDERAL GOVERNMENT GRANTED A TRACT OF THE RESERVATION ACQUIRED BY TREATY IN THAT YEAR. FROM ANTOINE OUILMETTE THE VILLAGE TAKES IT'S NAME. THE TRACT WAS ACQUIRED BY THE PIONEER FOUNDERS OF WILMETTE IN 1844.

WILMETTE HISTORICAL COMMISSION 1954

Plaque commemorating Antoine Ouilmette. In 1954, the Wilmette Historical Commission dedicated this plaque at the southeast corner of Lake Street and Michigan, a few hundred feet from the site of the Ouilmette cabin.

2

Pioneers to Pickle Packers
1840-1870

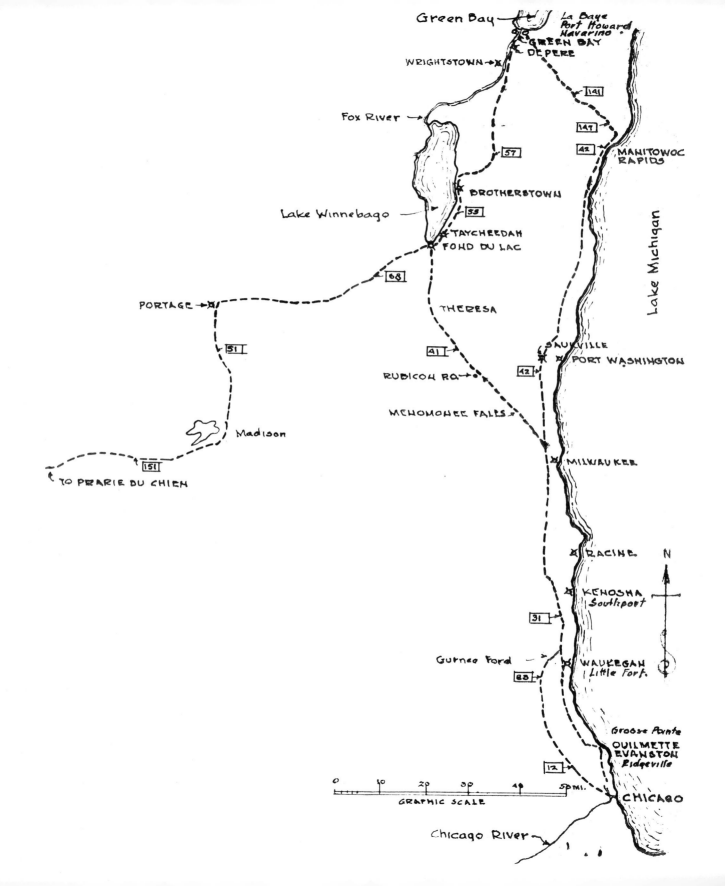

The Green Bay Trail. In the late 1820's, when little was known about the region north and west of the tiny settlement and fort on the banks of the Chicago River, a well-worn trail led north 14 miles to the point of land named Grosse Pointe by the sailors on Lake Michigan. When the Indians near Fort Howard at Green Bay grew restless and an uprising seemed imminent in the summer of 1827, the only route which could be followed between Fort Howard and Fort Dearborn was by water.

Then John H. Fonda, an adventurer and explorer who had come west from New York, blazed a trail to Fort Howard 240 miles north of Chicago, carrying dispatches and taking 30 days to cover the distance. The trail became a regular communications link between the two forts, and was called the Green Bay Trail. As settlements sprang up, the path was widened by wagons to become a rough road, and settlers built their cabins and frame houses along its length. The Green Bay Trail led in a northwestern direction from Rush Street to Rose Hill, then turned north along the sand ridge, now Ridge Avenue, Evanston. Known both as the Federal Road and Green Bay Trail, the route was the main artery for the development of Wilmette and its neighboring communities in the decades after the 1829 Treaty of Prairie du Chien.

When the Ouilmette family left their land to move west to Iowa, the Gross Point area was a region of thick forests, swamps, and Indian trails. The main north-south artery was the Green Bay Trail, which ran northward from Chicago's second Fort Dearborn along what is today Clark Street and Ridge Avenue in Evanston, then turned east in Wilmette along the lake shore. The Green Bay Trail linked the Prairie City with Little Fort (now Waukegan) and Fort Howard in Green Bay.

For the post runners who carried the mail when the weather was too bad for the sailing ships, the Trail's round trip took one month, much of the progress through dense forests, around deep ravines, and where the storm-lashed lake washed away sections, by detours. Along this early road, settlers were beginning to build their log cabins near the lake, and a few enterprising pioneer innkeepers opened taverns to accommodate the slowly growing stream of travelers who moved by stagecoach, horseback, and ox-drawn wagon.

In mid-August, 1836, a 21-year-old man named Alexander McDaniel walked northward from Chicago, then a village of 700. McDaniel had left his family farm at Painted Post, New York, arrived in Chicago in May, and discovered the beauty of the Grosse Pointe area. After passing Butterfield's Inn, then a house south of today's Graceland cemetery, he crossed the southern boundary of the future Evanston. There the tavern of Major Edward H. Mulford stood on Ridge

Alexander McDaniel, First Postmaster and Village Treasurer. Born in 1815 at Painted Post, New York, McDaniel traveled west to Chicago with a wagon train, arriving in May, 1836 at 21. He built a log cabin in Winnetka and in 1853, moved to Wilmette, living in the Joel Stebbins cabin at Linden and Sheridan until he built a house at Maple and Sheridan. When Wilmette was platted in 1869, McDaniel built a larger home at the southeast corner of Central and Wilmette Avenues. He was active in the real estate business, and served as postmaster for 19 years, and as a village trustee from 1872 to 1875. McDaniel died in 1898 and is buried at Rosehill Cemetery in Chicago.

Avenue near what is now St. Francis Hospital. Continuing north, McDaniel came to the Ouilmette cabin where, he recalled nearly 60 years later, he enjoyed "as fine a dinner with my hosts as could be got up by an American Family." Hiring an Indian guide, McDaniel continued his trip to visit friends living near the Des Plaines River. In late October he returned to the Grosse Pointe region and took a section of land near the present Chicago & North Western station at Elm Street, Winnetka. He built a cabin and lived a bachelor's life until he married Emeline Huntoon in November, 1842. In 1853, after buying land in Evanston and living for three years at Ridge Avenue and Church Street, the McDaniels moved to the Ouilmette Reservation, living in settler Joel Stebbins' cabin until they finished a house at the northeast corner of Maple Avenue and Sheridan Road.

As early as 1836, mail was delivered to Niles (then called "Dutchman's Point" because the trees of the forest tapered to a point in that German settlement) by

Map of Cook and DuPage Counties, 1851. Chicago boasted a population of 28,620, and Ridgeville was still to become Evanston. Settlements of early pioneers and tavern keepers are clearly indicated, as is the Green Bay & Chicago Road and "Cat'ic" church in the area which was to become Gross Point village in 1874. Note mileages to various Michigan points across Lake Michigan.

MAP
OF
THE COUNTIES OF
COOK AND DUPAGE
THE EAST PART OF
KANE AND KENDALL
THE NORTH PART OF
WILL,
State of Illinois,
Compiled by
JAMES H. REES,
Land Agent
CHICAGO, ILL.
1851.

SCALE.

Entered according to Act of Congress,
1851 by James H. Rees in the Cl..
of the District of Illinois.

Engraved & printed at Held. Mayer's

N 28° E 252 Miles to L.H. on Little Mantion
N 35° E 88 Miles to Grand Haven
N 53° 30 E 80 Miles to Kalamazoo River
N 74° E 61½ Miles to St. Josephs
S 84° 30 E 45 Miles to New Buffalo
S 25° E 38 Miles to Michigan City

20

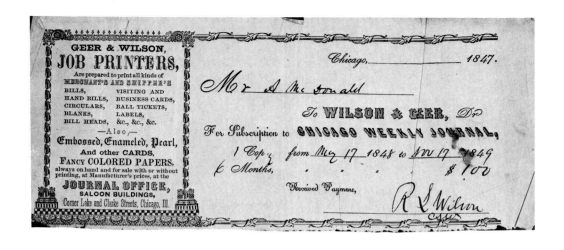

Receipt for Alexander McDaniel Newspaper Subscription, 1847. As a pioneer North Shore resident, Alexander McDaniel kept himself informed about events through an 18-month subscription to the Chicago Weekly Journal, then published at Clark and Lake Streets in Chicago.

stage coaches traveling from Chicago to Libertyville on the Milwaukee Plank Road. After Evanston was incorporated as a city in 1863, the first post office was opened in Colvin's store at the present location of Chicago Avenue and Davis Street, which served the early settlers along the Green Bay Trail.

Hard on the heels of McDaniel, Joel C. Stebbins moved into the abandoned cabin of Ouilmette in 1840. Because of the rapid erosion of the banks above Lake Michigan, Stebbins built his own cabin on higher ground at the southeast corner of present-day Linden Avenue and Sheridan Road. Still earlier, in 1837, Lombard Dusham came from Canada, bought 100 acres of land from Ouilmette for ten cents an acre, built a cabin near Ashland and Sheridan Road, and planted corn. Although little is known about Dusham, he was certainly a frugal pioneer; he salvaged timbers from the wreckage of the Lady Elgin to build a corn crib, after the ill-fated excursion steamer collided with the lumber ship Augusta off Winnetka in September, 1860.

In 1840 young John Gedney Westerfield, who became Wilmette's first president 32 years later, left Yonkers, New York, to visit the region, traveling from Buffalo by boat. So impressed was he with the possibilities of the Grosse Pointe area he returned to New York, sold his boat-building business, and returned in 1857 to buy 270 acres of farmland on the Lake Michigan shore. His land included the

long-vacant Ouilmette cabin, and Westerfield showed a true sense of history by preserving the cabin until 1865, when he had to raze it to keep the structure from washing into the lake. Some of the logs he saved were lost later, and the rest were used to build a shelter for his livestock.

During the decades of the 1850's and 1860's, Wilmette nearly became the pickle capital of the nation. In 1856, an energetic businessman of 38 named Squire Dingee left Westchester County, New York, to explore the Gross Point area with an eye towards starting a business there. Dingee, the older brother of Samuel Merritt Dingee, bought several hundred acres of land, most of it inside the present boundaries of Wilmette. Two years later, with brother Samuel's help, he was growing cucumbers and carting them to his own pickle plant in Chicago's Rose Hill section. By 1886, the enterprise was incorporated as the Squire Dingee Company; in 1924 it adopted the "Ma Brown" label. Early Wilmette's grocery stores proudly displayed large pickle barrels until 1900, when they started selling the product in the new-fangled glass jars.

To reinforce Wilmette's early claim to a pickle monopoly, John G. Westerfield was operating a small pickle factory near his home, probably the first such enterprise in the west. Even after he stopped making pickles, Westerfield developed a special strain of cucumber seed known into the early 1900's as "Westerfield's Chicago Cucumber Seed" and highly

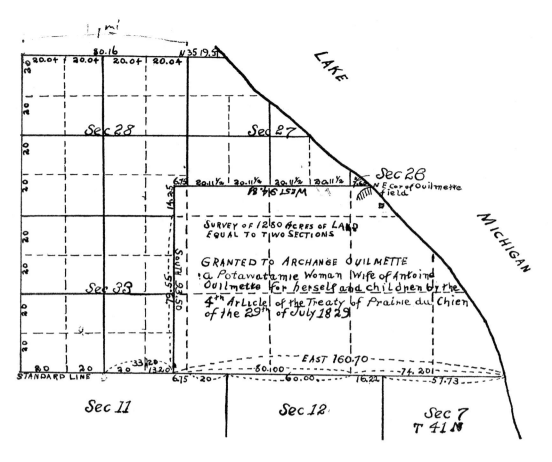

Drawing of the Ouilmette Reservation and additional sections. The drawing shows the survey started in the third quarter of 1840 and completed in April, 1842. The original plat was approved October 8, 1842. Drawing by James D. Kline.

prized by commercial growers.

In 1850, the thick forest along the lake shore was being cleared for dwellings, and a growing migration of German farmers was settling along what is now Ridge Road. The Skokie marshlands to the west were a mire even in dry weather, and the nearby peat bogs often caught fire, sending clouds of smoke across the region. In Ridgeville to the south, to become Evanston in a decade, there were fewer than 450 residents. That April, a group of settlers including many of the German farmers met at the home of John Garland in Winnetka, to organize a township government. To commemorate their homeland, the German settlers named the township New Trier, and elected James Hartrey as the first supervisor of the area's only governmental unit.

Wilmette's first schoolhouse, built of logs in 1847, was located east of Sheridan Road and south of Maple Avenue. In 1854, a small schoolhouse was built on the lake shore at Sheridan Road and Canterbury Court, the site marked by a plaque today. By 1863, there was a frame school east of Green Bay Road on the border of Evanston and Wilmette.

During the late 1840's, after United States President James K. Polk approved the transfer of Ouilmette's land in May, 1847, land speculators and settlers did a steady and profitable business in land sales; the interest rate for mortgages on the land sometimes was as high as 12 percent. In 1851, Alonzo Harmon and his wife sold 270 acres of lake-front land in the northeastern section of the Ouilmette Reservation to John Llewellin for $1,050, Llewellin soon selling the land to Solomon Dingee. In May, 1857, Mary J. Dennis sold 120 acres of land she had purchased from the government north of Elmwood Avenue to John Gage for $13,173, or about $100 an acre. When the Chicago and Milwaukee Railway — to become the Chicago and North Western — built a line to Waukegan in 1854, the growth of Wilmette was assured, although the main migration would not begin until after the terrible Chicago Fire of October 9, 1871. By 1869, a pattern of homes, stores and rough roadways had begun to emerge. It became the force for the next step, the incorporation of Wilmette as a village.

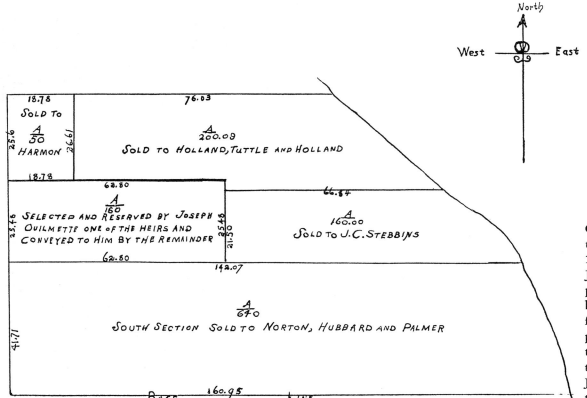

Copy of the Subdivision of the Ouilmette Reservation, 1844, The adaptation, by James D. Kline, shows the parts sold to land companies by the heirs, and was drawn from a certificate copy of the plat of the first subdivision of the Reservation. Note that the section belonging to Joseph Ouilmette was held at this time.

3
Gross Point:
New Trier's German Settlers

Everything is much easier for the farmer, more convenient, more care-free — There are no mountains to climb (and) when you step out of your door, you are at your work. . . We have no foresters and very little taxes. . . The trades are well paid: young men receive pay even when they are only apprentices. . . (Letter written in 1846 by Franz Joseph Hoffman to his uncle in Denn, Germany)

At about the time Antoine Ouilmette and his family were moving to Iowa from their cabin on the shores of Lake Michigan, a steady stream of German farmers from along the Rhine and Moselle Rivers in the district of Trier near Alsace and Luxembourg began to move into the area west of present-day Ridge Avenue. The area then known as Grosse Pointe (the final e's were dropped several years later) extended from Montrose Avenue and Graceland Cemetery in Chicago to what is now County Line Road in Highland Park.

The name Grosse Pointe came from the sharp bend in Lake Michigan north of the Northwestern University campus. In this chapter, the name "Gross Point" will be used to refer to the German-settled area west of Ridge Road in present Wilmette, although the Village itself was not incorporated until March, 1874.

These immigrants were hard-working farmers, deeply religious and primarily Catholic. They had left their farms in Germany, cutting all ties with relatives and friends to escape the oppression which plagued Germany and much of the European continent in the

Log Cabin built in 1840 by Bernard Kloepfer. Pictured in a 1903 photograph, the early Gross Point dwelling was located one and one-half miles west of the west boundary of the village, and is typical of the pioneer log houses of the period.

1830's and 1840's, and led to the Revolution of 1848. Crushing taxes, compulsory military service, despotic governments which denied freedoms to unify Germany's states, and the spectre of famine — all these factors played a part in the mass migration of freedom-loving Germans to America, the land of opportunity. Landing in the east, the immigrants came west in wagons, before the railroads built westward.

Typical of the Germans who came to Illinois and settled west of Ridge Avenue were Bartholomew Hoffmann, his wife, Anne Veronica, and their eight children. In June, 1844, the Hoffmanns left their home in Denn, near the city of Trier, and sailed to America, a trip which took more than two months. Arriving late that summer, they traveled overland to join their countrymen in Gross Point, and bought a 100-acre tract of land on Wilmette Avenue, between present-day Locust and Hunter Roads, for which they paid six dollars an acre. The land on which the family settled included part of the present site of Highcrest School. The eight children were Franz Joseph, Anna Catherine, Mary Elizabeth, John Augustine, Anna Marie, Mathias Joseph, Maria Veronica, and Anna Liftildes. In addition to the children there were Anna Catherine's husband, Johann Schmitz, and their daughter, Anna Maria Schmitz. On this land, Franz Joseph served as the first schoolmaster, teaching school in 1846 and 1847 to five pupils. On October 23, 1844, John Schaefer, son of Peter and Lena (Bleser) Schaefer, was the first white child born in Wilmette.

In 1846, the first post office in Grosse Pointe was established in the home of Evanston pioneer Major E. H. Mulford, at the present site of Ridge Avenue and Mulford Street in south Evanston (Evanston is planning to build a replica of the Mulford tavern as a historical restoration). At this time, the two final e's were dropped from the Gross Point name. Mail delivery was uncertain, particularly letters traveling the long distance to and from Germany, so the Hoffmann family kept copies of some of the letters they wrote to family in the old country. Unfortunately, records of Gross Point village from incorporation in 1874 to annexation by Wilmette in 1924 seem to have disappeared, so the Hoffmann letters are the primary early source of information about the area. George M. Huntoon was appointed the first postmaster of the new Gross Point post office, serving for two and a half years.

Discovered in a box by John Hoffmann, descendant of the Bartholomew Hoffmann family, the Hoffmann letters were translated from the German by his daughter Mary in the mid-1940's. In one letter, dated July 31, 1845, at Gross Point, Johann and Anna Catherine Schmitz replied to a letter written four months earlier from Germany, noting that "There are about forty land owners, proving that those who have settled here (Gross Point) are not all fools and idiots." Johann said that his sister-in-law Anna Maria "is a servant girl in Chicago and receives $53 wages a year — on Sunday, she is dressed like a lady and does not wish herself back in Germany."

His letter continued, "We can sell all our produce, large or small, in Chicago. The average price for a cow is $8.00 to $9.00; a yoke of oxen is $30.00; a horse, $30.00; a 200-pound hog, $4.00. . . A pound of beef costs $.04; pork, $.03; a pound of coffee,

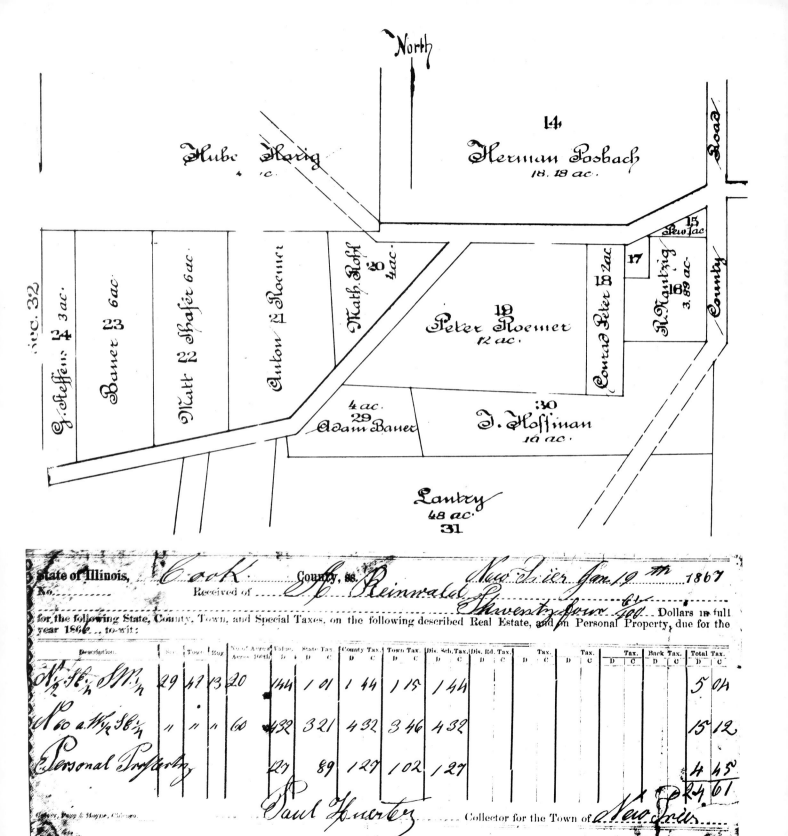

North

Sec. 32

14
Herman Posbach
18.18 ac.

Hube Maria
ac.

15
Sew ac.

17

R Rauting
3.89 ac.

16

J. Steffens 24 3ac.

Bauer 23 6ac.

Matt 22 Shafer 6ac.

Anton 21 Roemer

Math. Roff 20 4ac.

Conrad Peter 15 2ac.

Peter Roemer 19 12 ac.

4 ac. 29 Adam Bauer

30 J. Hoffman 10 ac.

Road

County

Lantry 48 ac. 31

State of Illinois, Cook County, ss.
No. Received of H. Reinwald New Trier Jan. 19th 1867 Twenty-four 61/100 Dollars in full for the following State, County, Town, and Special Taxes, on the following described Real Estate, and on Personal Property, due for the year 1866, to-wit:

Description.	Sec	Town	Rge	No of Acres Acres 100th	Value. D	D C	State Tax D C	County Tax D C	Town Tax D C	Dis. Sch. Tax. D C	Dis. Rd. Tax. D C	Tax. D C	Tax. D C	Tax. D C	Back Tax. D C	Total Tax. D C
N½ Se¼ SW¼	29	41	13	20	1 44		1 01	1 44	1 15	1 44						5 04
N 60 a W½ Se¼	"	"	"	60	4 32		3 21	4 32	3 46	4 32						15 12
Personal Property					1 27		89	1 27	1 02	1 27						4 45
																24 61

Paul Huertez _____ Collector for the Town of New Trier

478

28

J. B. Lauermann Dry Goods Store. Featuring a wide assortment of needs from the advertised boots and shoes to brooms and rakes, the store, pictured here in the 1880's or 1890's, stood on the west side of Ridge Avenue at Forest, where Mallinckrodt College is now located. The smaller building at the right is the original Lauermann's Tavern, built in the 1840's and identified in the Rees Map of Cook, DuPage, Kane and Kendall counties for 1851.

$.10; sugar, $.10; and 200 pounds of salt in a barrel, $1.75."

After noting that artisans were doing well, with a bricklayer earning 10 to 12 shillings (a shilling equaled about 12½ cents) and a wagon maker 6 to 8 shillings and room and board, Johann observed, "America is no land of perfection, where nothing is left to hate or wish for — such a land is nowhere. But, as I said before, here you can make a better living and get through life easier."

If the hard work of farming in the new land occupied the daylight hours, Gross Pointers were no less dedicated to their religious life, which combined both spiritual and temporal hours of relaxation. During the first years of their migration, the settlers depended upon priests from the Catholic diocese at Vincennes, Indiana, who rode the circuit.

In 1843 or 1844, they built the first church, a log cabin 24 by 30 feet just south of today's cemetery for St. Joseph's Church. In 1844, the See (a major division of the Catholic Church) of Chicago was established, and on November 21, 1845, the Rev. Gerhard H. Platke from Boston became the first pastor of the newly-founded St. Joseph's Church, which served a parish extending as far north as McHenry.

Almost two years later, in April 1847, Franz Joseph Hoffmann wrote to his uncle Michael: "On February, 1845, we had our first priest. On New Year's Day, 1847, he was transferred to Chicago and his place was vacant until March 9th when our second pastor, Rev. Fortman took his place." Evidently Father Fortman, from Munster in Westphalen, was a beloved leader, for Franz continues, "He is a true follower of the apostles and a disciple of our Lord. He

Gross Point pioneers Johann and Anna Lauermann. Anna, born in July, 1795, died in October, 1854. Johann B., born in 1788, died in June, 1847. This photograph is one of the very early examples of photography in America, and was probably taken not long before Johann's death.

is gentleness, love, patience and humility itself." Now the settlers could participate in Mass every day and, on Sunday, celebrate High Mass with a sermon,, singing the Latin and "Old German hymns" in the morning.

As the Gross Point settlement grew, the people expanded the log mission church, replacing it in 1849 with a larger frame building. In a letter dated December 13, 1857, John Augustin Hoffmann wrote that a frame church 30 by 90 feet had been completed, that wagonloads of people now came on Sunday "from near and far" to participate in "the beautiful church services" under the leadership of the Reverend Kopp, and that a public school had been opened; its teacher, Anton Meiler, was paid a salary of $200 a year, plus 25 cents a month per pupil.

In 1868, a young priest named Father William Netstraeter, born 25 years before in Westphalia, was ordained and said his first mass at St. Joseph's, serving as pastor from 1872 until 1923. Father Netstraeter became the leader in building a new St. Joseph's church, a stone building 50 by 120 feet, for which the farmers hauled the stone and sand from Chicago for weeks. During his dedicated career, the pastor was active not only as the parish leader, but also in Gross Point. Most significantly, he served largely Protestant Wilmette as village president twice, from 1886 to 1887, and again from 1890 to 1891, also serving as a Wilmette trustee and as a member of the first board of education of New Trier High School in 1899. His church, completed in 1869, stood until 1936, when the present church was built, completed in 1939.

On March 10, 1874, a group of residents met and incorporated the Village of Gross Point, under the general statutes of Illinois. To provide leadership for the settlement of 450 people, the first village election was held, and Adam Bauer was elected President; Reinard Nanzig, Village Clerk; and John Schaefer, the first child born in Gross Point (October 23, 1844), became the first Village Treasurer. Named as Trustees were Bauer, Joseph Bauer, Thomas Bohnen, John J. Bleser, Joseph Pasbach, and Maternas Schaefer. The boundaries of the original Gross Point were Hill Road and Winnetka Avenue on the north; the township line near Central Street, Evanston, on the south; a line approximately along the Indian Hill railroad station and Ridge Road on the east; and along Locust Road on the west.

Although almost no records of Gross Point are known to exist, the Revised Ordinances of the Village for 1906-1907 include some interesting insights into

Rev. William Netstraeter, pioneer Gross Point religious leader. Born in Westphalia in 1843, Father Netstraeter was ordained in 1868 and served as pastor of St. Joseph's Church for over 51 years, from 1872 until 1923.

Schiller's Corners, Circa 1870. In this badly faded photograph, the view is north along Ridge Road towards St. Joseph's Church on the right. A large group of Gross Point residents have assembled for the photograph, by an unknown pioneer photographer.

Law and Order in Gross Point, circa 1888. Officers Peter J. Schaefgen, left, and Joseph Engels were the settlement's first two policemen, charged, in addition to keeping the peace, with preventing cows from foraging in grocery stores. Both were born in Gross Point, Schaefgen in 1855 and Engels in 1860.

Threshing in Gross Point, circa 1900. While the steam thresher maintains a head of steam, farmers and families take a short break for a portrait on a hot summer day, dressed in the clothes of the time.

Gross Point Village "Execution." This photograph, taken on July 4, 1907, was a bit of Independence Day fun, despite the serious expressions of the "victims." Max Engels holds the pistol, and faces, from left, Joe Steffens, Ted Young, Joe Engels. Max Engels' son, Nick, holds the horse.

Old Gross Point Band, date unknown. Gross Point settlers combined a love of the land and religious devoutness with the German enjoyment of band music.

Huerter Legion Post, First Gross Point School. Named for the only Gross Point man to die in World War I, the Peter J. Huerter Post 669, American Legion, was organized in June, 1920. Members bought in 1946 the original two-room brick schoolhouse built in 1895 to serve 61 pupils and remodeled it extensively to use as a post meeting hall.

Gross Point Wedding, April, 1903. Celebrating the wedding of Susan Weinz and John Thalmann are representatives of the leading Gross Point families, including the Brauns, Schmitts, Engels, and Thalmanns. Contents of the steins held by Chris Braun and Matt Weber (right) are unknown.

Frank Ortegal's Gross Point Bakery. This undated photograph was probably taken about the turn of the century and shows St. Joseph's Church spire in the background. Note the Cracker Jack box used as a partition in the bakery wagon.

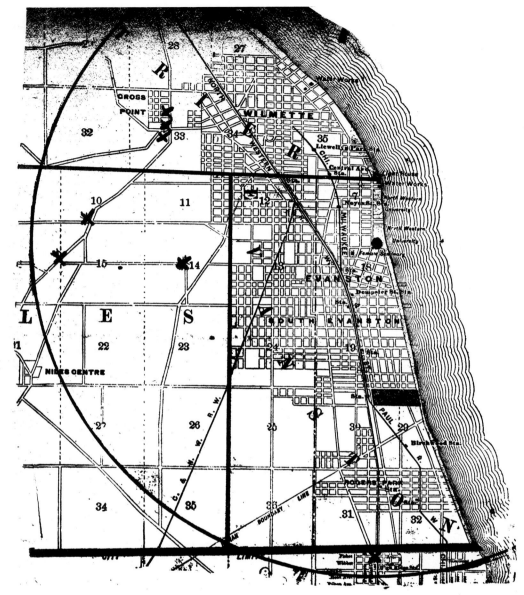

THE FOUR-MILE LIMIT.

The Circular Line is drawn with a four-mile radius, the University Hall being the Center of the Circle. The Crosses indicate the location of Saloons now in existence within the proscribed district. Township boundaries are indicated by straight black heavy lines.

The above map is very accurate in every detail, being taken from Rand, McNally's map of 1891. The map tells its own story better than columns of reading matter. May the information conveyed stir our people to the exigencies of the situation. The famous Gross Point saloons are within the proscribed district. When the case of the Gross Point saloons was before the courts some twenty years ago, the ruling was that the saloons were four miles distant by the nearest travelled road. Since that time new roads have been opened up, which bring the said saloons three and a quarter miles from the door of the university by good roads. Verily, there is work for a Citizen's League to do. Let us have a Citizen's League. Not a Rogers Park League, not an Evanston League, not a Wilmette League, but a league that will include every respectable . . .

Gross Point saloons target for Citizens League. An 1893 adaptation from an 1891 Rand McNally map, showing saloons in Gross Point, Niles Centre (Center, later Skokie) and the north limits of Chicago. At this time, they were within the circle, or four-mile limit from Northwestern University, a violation of the ordinance which had stated that no liquor should be sold closer than that distance from the university. The accompanying article, publication unknown, urged the formation of a Citizens League of "every respectable citizen within the four-mile limit" to campaign for the abolition of the offending saloons.

Schallick's Tavern, about 1903. Located on the southwest corner of Ridge Road and Wilmette Avenue, Schallick's was one of some 15 taverns in the Gross Point village area during its half-century before incorporation with Wilmette. Pictured, left to right, are patrons William Klinge, Mike Loutsch, and John Loutsch. The bartender behind the bar is Joe Rengel. Other bartender is unidentified.

the problems which had to be met by law at that time. Gross Point had grown large enough to almost double the number of trustees elected in 1874; add a Village attorney, Louis J. Pierson, and a comptroller, Gangolf Sesterhenn; and to have a Board of Local Improvements staffed by Joseph Heinzen, John Mick, and Peter Schaefgen, and a Board of Health, whose four members included Heinzen (also Village President), Schaefgen, Sesterhenn, and Dr. J. P. Koerper, M.D. Albert Zeutschel was police magistrate and John J. Huerter was Village Fire Marshall.

Appointive offices included the Street Commissioner (paid $2 a day for time actually spent in his job) and a Poundmaster to capture and care for stray animals, collecting costs from owners within forty-eight hours, or taking delinquent animal owners to court after that allotted time.

JOE SEGER'S GROVE,

Near Wilmette Station, 14 Miles North of Chicago.

LAID OUT IN RESIDENCE LOTS.

This tract of land is very nicely situated, 14 miles from Chicago, on the Milwaukee Railroad, near Wilmette Station, and about one mile distant from the Lake. It is high and dry, gravel ground, nearly covered with trees. Good water can be obtained by digging wells about ten feet deep.

It joins the new catholic brick Church and Schoolhouse and is about 10 minutes distant from the Wilmette Depot.

The lots are first-rate residence lots for persons, which have their business in Chicago and are looking for a nice and cheap home.

Three trains leave the Wilmette Depot for Chicago in the morning, between 6 and 8 and three trains leave Chicago in the eve., betw. 5 and 7 o'clock.

The lots are from 50 to 74 feet wide and from 177 to 185 feet deep with an alley to each lot. Prices range from $475 to $500 on easy terms.

These lots sell very rapidly and on some of them are houses already erected, and more than half of them are sold.

For information call on

~~Mrs. SEGER,~~ ~~Propr, 477 North Clark Street, Chicago.~~
PETER J. HAND, 637 N. Clark St. and 120 Washington St.
JOHN SCHAEFER, Near Wilmette Station, (Seger's Grove)

Der obengenannte Grove ist vor Kurzem durch den Eigenthümer in Bauplätze ausgelegt. Dieselben sind von 50 bis 74 Fuß breit und 177 bis 185 Fuß tief, mit einer Alley hinter jeder Lot. Die Preise für diese Bauplätze sind von ~~$400~~ bis ~~$500~~ 475–500 je nach der Lage und Größe derselben. Die Bedingungen sind sehr günstig.

Der Platz ist ausgezeichnet gelegen, ist ungefähr 14 Meilen von Chicago an der Milwaukee Eisenbahn, eine Meile vom See, liegt hoch und trocken, hat Kiesboden und ist mit Bäumen bestanden. Ein Brunnen von nur 10 Fuß Tiefe liefert vorzügliches Wasser. In unmittelbarer Nähe ist die katholische Backsteinkirche und das Schulhaus, kaum 10 Minuten entfernt ist das Wilmette Depot.

Dieser Platz eignet sich vorzüglich für Chicagoer Geschäftsleute, welche eine billige Baustelle suchen. Morgens zwischen 6 und 8 Uhr gehen 3 Eisenbahnzüge nach Chicago und Abends, zwischen 5 und 7 Uhr, gehen gleichfalls 3 Eisenbahnzüge von Chicago nach Wilmette.

Die Bauplätze verkaufen sich sehr gut und sind schon über die Hälfte verkauft.

Näheres zu erfragen bei

~~Frau Seger, Eigenthümerin, No. 477 Nord Clark Str.~~
Peter J. Hand, 637 Nord Clark Straße und 120 Washington Str.
John Schäfer, nahe Wilmette Station, (Seger's Grove.)

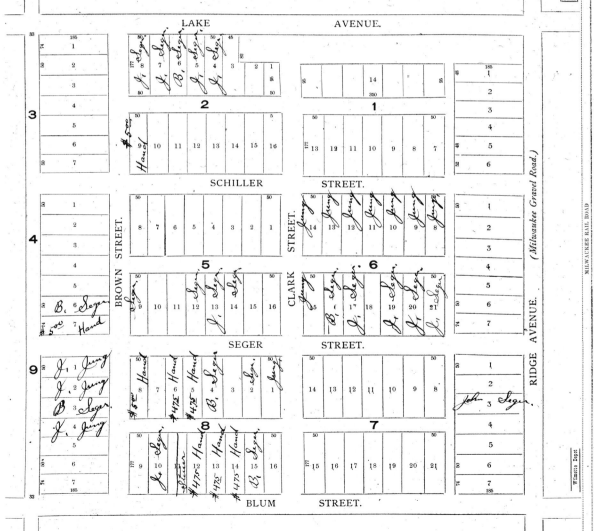

Joe Seger's Grove
Land Promotion Handbill.
Undated promotional
handbill is printed in both
English and German, and
includes lot price increases
entered in pen. Area is
south of Lake Avenue and
west of Ridge Road.
Schiller is now an Avenue,
Seger Street was changed
to Birchwood Avenue, and
Blum Street became
Washington Avenue. More
than half the lots have
already been sold, with
owner's names added.

**Braun Family of Gross Point,
Circa 1900.** Pioneers of the
Gross Point region, the
Brauns lived at 728 Illinois
Road when photograph was
taken. People are
unidentified, except for Anna
Braun at right.

The growing number of automobiles prompted a
short chapter in the ordinances. The speed limit was
eight miles an hour, and automobiles and "autocars"
had to be equipped with "an alarm bell or gong of not
less than four (4) inches in diameter, or with an
automobile horn" which was to be sounded at street
crossings and in other necessary situations. Section 3
provided that should a car approach a horse being
driven or ridden, and if the horse were "about to
become frightened," the car driver "must come to a
full stop" until the horse had passed. To put teeth
into the ordinance, the minimum fine was set at the
then not trivial sum of $25 and the maximum at
$200, perhaps five or six times that amount today.

Cyclists at night had to have a light, and were
forbidden to ride on any sidewalk. The ordinances also
reflected the problem of stray animals, from dogs and
cats to horses, bulls, oxen, pigs, sheep, goats, and
other farm animals. Dramshops or saloons — an
important place of relaxation for the hardworking
Gross Point farmer — were strictly controlled, with
licenses of $500 a year, closing hours from midnight
to 5 a.m., and no sales to minors or incompetents.

Many of the Gross Point ordinances were
concerned with fines for polluting water, keeping
swine closer than 300 feet to a house, or slaughtering
animals for sale without a permit. Special ordinances
allowed the Chicago Telephone Company to furnish
telephone service to residents, and the Evanston
Electric Illuminating Company had the similar right to
provide and service not less than 10 arc lamps at
strategic points, including intersections, at a cost of
$60 a year per lamp.

In April, 1919, with Wilmette to the east a

Gross Point Sunday Picnic, After 1900. The Gross Point band will provide music for the outing, which includes small children and everyone in their best Sunday finery. Location unknown, but probably on the lake front.

growing and prospering suburb, the Gross Point citizens voted to dissolve the municipal government. But not until the Gross Point Village Hall was sold to the Hoffmann brothers in October, 1923, to pay the Village debts, could this first step towards annexation be accomplished. In 1919, America passed the Prohibition (18th) Amendment, prohibiting the manufacture and sale of alcoholic beverages, a death blow to the Gross Point saloons and a considerable part of the village's business prosperity.

In January, 1924, some citizens made an attempt to reorganize Gross Point in a referendum, but the attempt was defeated in a special election. That April, the part of Gross Point east of present-day Illinois Road voted to join Wilmette, and within two years most of the balance of the original Gross Point village was annexed. It is interesting to note that a majority of the men opposed dissolving the Village, and a majority of the women (allowed by Illinois law to vote in separate balloting for some proposals, though not in national elections) supported the step. In 1924, Gross Point was no more, having become the western section of Wilmette.

4
Village in the Forest

42

Map of 1868 Land Holdings.
Dutch Settlement Road extended
from Evanston to Gross Point, and
part of the road is present Prairie
Avenue. Drainage Commissioners'
Road today is the Wilmette Avenue -
Tenth Street route to Plaza Del
Lago. Section Line Road was the
north border of the Ouilmette lands,
and today is Elmwood Avenue.

On June 1, 1868, Asahel Gage, one of the four sons of John Gage, wrote a letter to his father, then living in Vineland, New Jersey, which sheds light on what was perhaps the most important early step to develop Wilmette.

In 1857, John Gage had purchased 118 acres of densely wooded land north of present-day Elmwood Avenue, an area extending from Lake Michigan to the Chicago and Milwaukee (now North Western) Railway tracks. Just three years earlier, the Chicago and Milwaukee had expanded its route northward, laying tracks as far as Waukegan, and making stops in what would become Evanston to pick up and discharge passengers. The first accommodation train made a run to Waukegan over wooden rails on January 20, 1855, covering the 36 miles in three hours. The train was a two-car affair, with a baggage car and coach with 12 passengers.

Before quoting from Asahel Gage's letter, brief mention should be made of what had happened earlier to pave the way for the Gage land acquisition.

Although the United States government issued the patent to the Ouilmette children in 1842, giving them permission to sell the land granted by the Treaty of Prairie du Chien in 1829, a number of sales were made before that date. In 1835, the Ouilmette family sold the south 640 acres of the Reservation to Nelson R. Norton, Allen P. Hubbard and Isaac K. Palmer for $1,100.

Concerned that the theft of timber was ruining their inherited lands, the Ouilmette children were anxious to sell and sell quickly. After May 14, 1847, when President James K. Polk gave his official approval for the land sales, both residents and land speculators began to buy, and often resell, parcels of land. As Herbert B. Mulford notes in his booklet "Frontiers of Old Wilmette," the original Ouilmette Reservation was expanded as early as 1840, when Mary Dennis bought 18.78 acres north of Elmwood Avenue. The following year, she bought 102.98 acres from the government and another 84.54 acres from John S. Clark, selling about 120 acres in May, 1857, to John Gage. There were many other transactions, but these sales were the chief means of expanding the area to become Wilmette beyond the boundaries of the original Ouilmette Reservation.

In his 1868 letter to the patriarch of the Gage family, son Asahel reported:

"Last Saturday, Henry (Henry H. Gage, his brother) and I went out to the site of the proposed station of Wilmett; the name was proposed by H. W. Blodgett (a judge from Waukegan who will be mentioned later in this chapter). . . the Depot is located just halfway between Evanston and Winnetka and two miles from each. . . The Rail Road Company have agreed to build a platform and establish a flag station and the parties interested are to build the Station House. . ."

His letter also discussed strategy in paying a part of the cost of a road and drainage ditch as a move beneficial to the Gage property holdings if the other "Wilmett"

Gage Family, Owners of Wilmette North of Elmwood Avenue. Seated, left to right, are Portia Kellog Gage; her husband, John, and son Asahel. Standing are the other three sons, Henry H. Augustus N., and John Portius. Date of photograph is unknown.

landowners would, in return, help build roads. But the important point is that if Wilmette were to attract settlers, regular rail transportation between Chicago and the area was essential. With a station, trains would stop in both directions and serve as a means of fast transportation, linking Chicago and the settlements to the north.

In 1869, a group of five men — Alexander McDaniel, Henry A. Dingee, Simon V. Kline, John G. Westerfield, and Judge Henry W. Blodgett of Waukegan — formed a land syndicate. Judge Blodgett was to receive a one-eighth interest in their profits, in return for using his influence as an advisor to the Chicago and Milwaukee Railroad, to add the as-yet unorganized village to regular railroad train stops.

That year, John G. Westerfield platted "Wilmette Village," the name suggested by Judge Blodgett as the anglicized version of pioneer settler

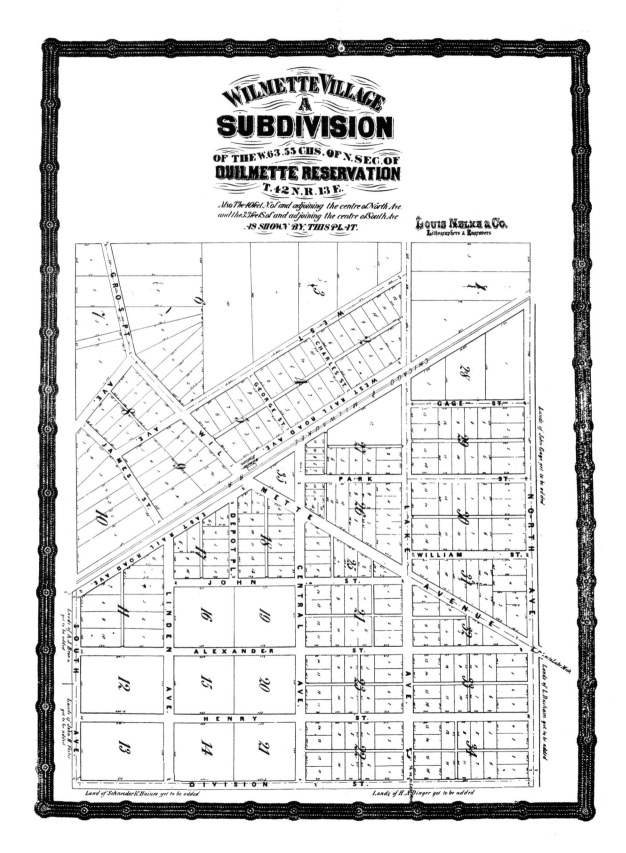

Original 1869 Plat of "Wilmette Village." This plat, reportedly made by surveyor John G. Westerfield, included an area of about 525 acres. Wilmette Avenue, Lake Avenue, and Central Avenue are unchanged, but many of the plat's street names are now numbered streets.

Ouilmette. Westerfield then began to lay out the streets, and the small syndicate set in motion the start of a land promotion program, to induce settlers to come and settle, building homes which would assure the growth of the tiny settlement centered around the depot. Finally, as the village took form, Alexander McDaniel and Henry Dingee joined to build, for $700, that first station of wood, which went into service sometime in 1871.

Although original records are missing, the first wooden depot apparently burned at its location on the west side of the tracks, just north of Wilmette Avenue and east of Rail Road Avenue (now Green Bay Road: see map), and directly opposite the present Crossroads Restaurant. Perhaps the Chicago Fire of October, 1871, whose terrible glow could be seen clearly by Wilmette's early families, emphasized the need to build a more substantial station in the minds of the developers.

A group of 10 of the developers agreed to collect subscriptions to build a new brick depot, costing almost $3,500, under the supervision of a building committee including "A. McDaniel, J. G. Westerfield, and C. D. Paul, according to plans and specifications approved by said Railway company." The agreement, dated December 1, 1873, set forth the amounts paid by the subscribers, who included McDaniel; Westerfield, then president of the village; Henry A. Dingee, a syndicate member and brother-in-law of Westerfield; and two members of the Gage family. Records do not explain why the agreement was dated almost seven months after the May 4, 1873, issue of the *Chicago Sunday Times*, which carried the following news story:

"Willmet (sic) is the next station beyond Evanston and about 14 miles from the city. The major portion of the town was once the property of

John Gedney Westerfield.
Wilmette's first president,
elected on the seventh ballot
on November 8, 1872, was
noted for his hospitality to
travelers. He first visited
the area in 1847, traveling
from Buffalo to Chicago by
boat, on a business mission
for Henry A. Dingee, and
shortly thereafter, bought
270 acres of land in the
northwest section of the
Ouilmette Reservation.

**Samuel S. Dingee, Pickle
Magnate and President.**
Moving to Wilmette in the
1870's, he served as the
fourth village postmaster
from 1893 to 1908, and in
1905, initiated mail carrier
service. From 1893 to 1895,
he was 12th Wilmette president.
Dingee joined his father,
Samuel M. Dingee, in the
pickle manufacturing business
in Evanston, which later
became the Squire Dingee
Pickle Company at the
North Western Railroad's
Clybourn Avenue station,
and finally, the Ma Brown
Pickle Company. In 1915,
Dingee moved to Wausau,
Wisconsin, to set up the S. S.
Dingee & Sons Pickle Company.
He died in that city in October,
1947, at 86.

Alexander McDaniel, an old Irishman, who still
exercises a sort of paternal vigilance over the
locality. The depot at this place is quite a
pretentious affair, and said to be the finest on the
entire line of the road. The general lay of the land
is fair, and averages about 30 feet above the lake.
The town census claims 300 inhabitants, and the
vigilant reportorial eye discerned about 60
pleasantly situated residences. The town was laid
out in 1871, when the depot was built. Since then
it has enjoyed a steady growth, and more
prosperous days are in store. A union church is
now building at a cost of $6,000 and will be
completed in a few months. . . Property in bulk is
valued at $500 per acre, while that divided into
lots sells at prices ranging from $5 to $10 a front
foot, within a reasonable distance from the
station..."

Although the land developers and early pioneer
leaders of the area had platted Wilmette Village, and
evidently had built the brick depot months before the
date of the subscription agreement, the settlement at
that time was still a smaller part of New Trier Township,
without its own government or officials. Late in the
summer of 1872, a group of the leaders began to meet
in the home of Andrew T. Sherman, at 1136 Greenleaf
Avenue. Sherman was a great-grandson of Roger
Sherman, one of the signers of the Declaration of
Independence. On August 15, 1872, 42 citizens voted in
an election at the depot to create the Village of
Wilmette. Thirty-seven voted for the proposal, four
voted against, and one vote was blank. After several
preliminary meetings to discuss the organization of a
formal village government, on November 9, 1872, the

Chicago and North-Western RAILWAY.

TIME CARDS

— OF THE —

CHICAGO & NorthWestern RAILWAY.

In Effect January 7th, 1874.

| No. 4. | 1874. | February. |

Depot, corner Canal and Kinzie Streets, Chicago.
GOING NORTH.

Dist.	Time	STATIONS.	† Mail.	Express †Pass.	Express †Pass.	D Night Pass.
	h. m.	Le. CHICAGO............	8.00 AM	9.30 AM	5.00 PM	11.00 PM
2.5	......	" City Limits Junc....	8.12 "	9.42 "	5.12 "	*11.20 "
5.3	......	" Belle Plaine.........	8.20 "	9.48 "	5.18 "	*11.33 "
5.8	......	" Ravenswood.......	§ 8.21 "	9.50 "	5.19 "	*11.34 "
7.7	......	" Rosehill............	8.25 "	9.53 "	§ 5.23 "	*11.40 "
9.1	......	" Rogers' Park.......	8.26 "	9.55 "	5.25 "	*11.43 "
10.2	......	" Calvary.............	8.31 "	9.57 "	* 5.28 "	*11.49 "
10.8	......	" South Evanston....	8.33 "	9.59 "	* 5.29 "	*11.52 "
11.8	.32	" EVANSTON........	8.36 "	10.02 "	5.31 "	11.55 "
13.1	......	" North Evanston....	8.39 "	*10.05 "	* 5.34 "	*12.02 AM
14.0	......	" Wilmette...........	§ 8.42 "	*10.07 "	5.37 "	12.06 "
16.5	......	" Winnetka...........	8.50 "	*10.12 "	5.42 "	12.18 "
17.5	......	" Lake Side..........	8.52 "	*10.14 "	5.44 "	*12.21 "
18.9	......	" Glencoe............	8.57 "	*10.17 "	5.46 "	12.28 "
22.9	......	" HIGHLAND PARK	9.07 "	10.25 "	5.55 "	12.47 "
24.2	......	" Highwood..........	§ 9.11 "	*10.28 "	* 5.57 "	*12.53 "
28.0	1.07	" LAKE FOREST....	9.21 "	10.37 "	6.05 "	1.10 "
30.1	......	" Rockland...........	9.26 "	*10.41 "	6.10 "	1.20 "
35.6	1.28	" WAUKEGAN......	9.45 "	10.58 "	6.28 "	1.45 "
39.9	......	" Benton.............	9.54 "	*11.06 "	* 6.37 "	2.10 "
44.9	......	" State Line..........	§10.05 "	*11.17 "	* 6.47 "	§ 2.32 "
51.4	2.00	" KENOSHA.........	10.20 "	11.30 "	7.00 "	3.01 "
60.2	2.18	" RACINE JUNC....	10.41 "	11.48 "	7.22 "	3.40 "
61.7	2.26	" RACINE...........	10.49 "	11.56 "	7.30 "	4.00 "
64.3	......	" Ives Station........	*10.54 "	*12.01 PM	* 7.35 "	* 4.10 "
70.1	......	" County Line........	11.08 "	*12.12 "	§ 7.48 "	§ 4.30 "
75.3	......	" Oak Creek.........	11.21 "	*12.22 "	7.59 "	4.47 "
78.2	......	" Buckhorn..........	*11.28 "	*12.29 "	* 8.05 "	* 4.58 "
80.6	......	" St. Francis.........	§11.35 "	*12.33 "	8.10 "	* 5.07 "
82.9	......	" Elizabeth Street....	11.40 "	12.38 "	8.15 "	* 5.15 "
85.0	3.15	Ar. MILWAUKEE.....	11.50 AM	12.45 PM	8.30 PM	5.30 AM

* Trains do not stop.   § Trains stop on signal.   D Daily.
† Daily except Sunday.

MILWAUKEE DIVISION.

C&NW RR Depot, Circa 1875. Built after the original wooden depot burned, the brick building cost nearly $3,500, and was paid for by 10 subscribers, part of the Wilmette development group. Alexander McDaniel supervised construction. Timetable above shows an average running time from Chicago to Wilmette of about 42 minutes. In 1875 the fare to Chicago was 11 cents.

trustees of the Village of Wilmette met officially for the first time. Sherman was chosen temporary chairman, and B. M. Munn temporary secretary. The group elected John G. Westerfield as the first president on the seventh ballot. Alexander McDaniel was elected the village treasurer, Charles A. Vail clerk, and Mathias A. Gedney was appointed street commissioner and constable.

Even before Wilmette's founding fathers met to elect its first officers, land values in the beautiful wooded area along the lake were quickly rising, as the developers began to interest families in coming here to live. In 1869, land in the Wilmette area east of Rail Road Avenue (now Green Bay) sold for $150 an acre. A year later, the price had risen 33 percent to $200 an acre. After the first platting, land for sale was offered in block units, which in 1871 sold for from $2 to $3 a front foot.

Visualize the Wilmette of the early 1870's, at the time the trustees elected the village's first officers. Wilmette was heavily wooded and a thick forest east of Division (now Eighth Street) to the lake. There were no paved streets — early settlers traveled on paths or dirt trails. Water was pumped from wells or caught in rain barrels, the pump water used for cooking and the soft rain water for washing.

From the early days, most of the settlers worked in Chicago and carried oil lanterns to the depot in the morning, left them there during the day, and picked them up at night to light their way home. In 1875, the one-way train fare to Chicago was 11 cents, and the ride to the Chicago depot took about 30 minutes.

Life in the village during the early years was far from easy. In a letter written in 1935 to the Wilmette Old Settler's Association, Julia Kirk, then living in Newton Center, Massachusetts, with her daughter, recalled:

"We came to Wilmette in April, 1877. That was the spring that Henry A. Dingee's mortgages came due, and half of the people gave up their places and went back to the city. It was a cold, wet spring, and our house seemed damp and forlorn. There was nothing to be seen from the windows but bare trees and bushes, except in front, where we could see our neighbor's house across the street (Mrs. Kirk, her husband, Rufus, and their four children lived at 1044 Forest Avenue until 1915). Forest Avenue was only a road then, grass grown, with a wagon track in the middle and a very deep ditch on the south side.

"Soon after arriving in the village I went to the store, and it was The Store. A small grocery, with the post office on one side. Henry Kinney was the proprietor. When I asked for vegetables and fruit he said they never have kept those things, as everybody had a garden and there was no demand for them. I then went to the meat market, a much smaller store, where Baptist Mueller told me he butchered most of his meat in his back yard."

Julia Kirk was 25 when she came to their Forest Avenue house.

**Andrew T. Sherman House,
Circa 1872.** Birthplace of the
Village of Wilmette, the house
at 1136 Greenleaf Avenue no
longer exists.

Andrew T. Sherman, Village President and Trustee. The great-grandson of Roger Sherman, one of the signers of the Declaration of Independence, Sherman joined the Gold Rush and in 1850, lost his left leg in a steamer boiler explosion. After serving in the Civil War with the army from the start of the war, he worked for seven years in the Chicago office of the U.S. Commissioner. Sherman came to Wilmette in 1871, and was a member of the first village board, president from 1874-1875, and a trustee for three years. He died in Chicago in 1901 and was 80 at his death.

That fall, a daughter, Harriet, was born, to join her older brother, Eugene. Julia Kirk recalled the time when both babies caught colds and was told by their only neighbors, William and Henrietta Panushka at 1041 Forest, that there was a young doctor near the railroad named Byron C. Stolp, but that "no one ever went to him." Rufus Kirk did not own a horse and buggy, but walked to the doctor's house and brought him back, to cure the children. When the Kirks found that Dr. Stolp kept a cow for fresh milk, they decided to stay in Wilmette, instead of returning to Chicago, and during the 38 years her family lived in Wilmette, Julia Kirk recalled:

> "We saw this little, struggling village, with empty houses, dark streets and wooden sidewalks change to an up-to-date suburb with electric lights, paved streets, telephones, automobiles, a bank, a moving picture house, blocks and blocks of stores and hundred of beautiful homes."

Another Wilmette pioneer who recalled the early years was J. Melville Brown, who later built the Brown Building on the east side of Wilmette Avenue north of Central, and was active as a Wilmette businessman for many years. In 1918, he wrote his recollections of Wilmette, in so vivid a style that much of the letter is quoted here:

> "One of my earliest recollections is of following a wagon, filled with household goods, from our home in Evanston, through a beautiful forest to Wilmette. It was 1867, so I must have been four years old. There were five of us children at that time, and there not being room in the wagon for all, some of us waited behind, I being the youngest of the brood to walk. There were glimpses of the lake along the way to add to the

Mathias Anderson Gedney, Wilmette Planner and Police Magistrate. Born in Clarkstown, New York, Gedney went to sea at 14 aboard the U.S.S. Constitution, and by age 21 had sailed around the world three times. In 1856, he came from New York with his wife and small daughters to LaCrosse City, Wisconsin, and in 1863, left for a return to New York. After stopping to visit his cousin, John G. Westerfield in the Ouilmette settlement, Gedney decided to settle here, and went into business with Westerfield in the Northwestern Pickle Works, later joining Samuel M. Dingee. After assisting in the clearing of forests and in laying out the streets, and in drainage ditching and bridging for Wilmette, he served as police magistrate of the village from 1873 to 1877, and as a trustee of the first Wilmette board in 1872.

quiet, primitive beauty.

"For some time we did not meet any people, did not see any habitations on the way; but finally the first house sighted was a small one made of logs. . . now long since rebuilt and enlarged to the present Bockius residence at the southeast corner of Central and 11th Street . . . many said this had been the site of an Indian camp.

"Land was cheap and could be had for almost the asking; and my father immediately started building a little home for us on the very ground where the Masonic Temple now stands. My father's land ran from the alley to 10th Street and back to a depth of 300 feet. For many years no lot was less than 200 feet wide.

"The little settlement we had come to had fewer than a dozen homes; and was bounded, I would say, by Lake Avenue, Tenth Street, Greenleaf Avenue and the railroad tracks.

"The early large land owners were the Westerfields, Alexander McDaniel, the Gage family, the Dushams, Mahoneys and Henry Dingee of New York. Mr. Henry Dingee was reputed a millionaire, and excited both envy and respect on his annual visits to the village. He once had a very neat fence built around the triangle bounded by Central Avenue, Wilmette Avenue and 11th Street, and he promised to sometime donate it to the village for a park, but his heart failed him and he sold it later for real money.

"When we first came here in 1867, I am sure there was no school, no church, no store, no train which stopped at Wilmette! A little later one train

Wilmette's Pioneer Doctor, Byron C. Stolp. Born at Empire, Illinois, January 27, 1849, Dr. Stolp graduated in 1872 from Bennett Medical College, Chicago, and came to Wilmette in 1874, after marrying Carrie Graves of Wheaton and doctoring in New Castle, Indiana. He practiced medicine for 43 years, a highly popular citizen and active in civic affairs. His sons Rufus Byron and Harold Edgar were also doctors, Rufus practicing for many years in Wilmette. Dr. Stolp was killed in an automobile accident in November, 1917, en route to visit a patient.

a day each way did stop here; but even then I remember that when my brother Gilbert and I wanted very much to see the big city fourteen miles away, and to buy there a birthday gift for our mother, we walked all the way to Chicago because the train fare would have so depleted the little fund we had saved for the gift.

"The first store in Wilmette, and the only one for some time, was owned by Mr. Henry Kinney, and was located on what is now Green Bay Road, half way between Central and Wilmette Avenues. Mr. Kinney sold us our groceries, was station agent, postmaster, express agent, Village Treasurer, and general confidant and friend of the needy!

"The old coal stove in the rear of the store was a meeting place, and the starting point of many a story or bit of gossip. . . while neighbors waited for Mr. Kinney's cry 'All up, all out!' Meanwhile, the cracker barrel had suffered.

"One vivid memory is of watching, in awe and wonder, for many hours, a great expanse of lurid sky to the south of us. It was October of 1871. Our elders were apprehensive for they knew a terrible fire must be raging somewhere not very far away. There was no radio to tell us about it; even the telephone had not been invented then! We had no telegraph station in Wilmette, and only that one train a day!

"In the woods to the north, before Kenilworth was laid out and drained, water often stood high like a marsh — and in winter turned to ice. Then the night skating of the young people in and out among the silhouetted trees, holding aloft their flaming flares, was a vision to remember.

Records of The Board of Trustees of The Village of Wilmette

Wilmette Nov 8th 1872

At the first meeting of the Board of Trustees of the Village of Wilmette at the residence of A T Sherman on the 8th of November A D 1872 Mr A T Sherman was chosen temporary Chairman and B M Munn was appointed temporary Secretary

On Motion the Trustees proceeded to elect a President of the Board by ballot - Upon the 1st 2nd 3d 4th & 6th ballot there was no choice. Neither Candidate at any time having a majority of all the votes cast On the 7th ballot John S Westerfield received a plurality of all the votes cast and was duly elected and declared President of the Board of Trustees of the Village of Wilmette

On motion Alexander McDaniel was chosen Treasurer of the Village — On Motion Charles A Vail was appointed Village Clerk and on Motion M A Gedney was duly appointed Street Commissioner and Constable of said Village

On Motion Messrs Alex McDaniel and Chas T Boggs were appointed a Committee to select a suitable Official Seal with an appropriate device for said Village Corporation

On Motion Board adjourned to meet at same place Tuesday coming next

Signed B M Munn Clerk Pro Tem

Village Seal. Chosen by committee of Charles Boggs and Alexander McDaniel after first meeting of Trustees. Village Charter was issued September 19, 1872.

North Shore Baseball League, 1900-1904. Photograph, taken in 1901 or 1902, identifies players: Top row, from left - Dr. Walter Swarthout, pitcher and second base; Henry Gage, right field; Clarence Snyder, center field; John Davenport, left field; Frank Paul, first base. Bottom row, from left: Jack Farley, third base; W. Sewell Musson, catcher; J. Harrison Musson, pitcher and second base; and Walter Kammerdiener, shortstop.

Minutes of Board of Trustees First Meeting, November 8, 1872.

"We all had a well for drinking water, and a cistern for soft water; and it was often necessary to prime the pump in summer, and to thaw it out with hot water in winter. Songs about the Old Town Pump or the Old Oaken Bucket were very familiar and greatly appreciated. I might add, germs and microbes were an unknown quantity in those days in spite of which fact we were a healthy lot. We had frequent droughts drying our wells and cisterns and were compelled to haul water from the springs along the Gross Point Rd. or from the lake, spilling half in getting up the steep banks.

"For years the village scarcely extended east of Eighth Street or north of Lake Avenue. I well remember the advent of Mr. George Rogers on Forest Avenue and the interest excited among the boys by the only daughter, and the rigging of a 'tick tack' against the front window to frighten her. The tables were turned, however, by Mr. Rogers appearing on the scene with a shotgun, and some of the boys did not stop running until they reached North Evanston.

"Our roads were dirt or corduroy lined by deep ditches to carry the surplus rains. The old plank sidewalks were continually getting out of repair and were responsible for many a hard fall. The street lamps were of the oil burning kind, and few and far between. A request for a lamp in some benighted section caused heated discussions at the village meetings. Each household had its supply of lanterns always carried on dark nights and a procession headed to some public gathering reminded one of a lot of gigantic fireflies. There was a lot of genuine sociability displayed when we gathered about the warm stove to light up for the homeward journey. No doubt about it, the winters were colder and the snows deeper then than now, and the writer well remembers the many cords of hard knotty wood he had to dig from deep snow mounds each winter to keep the long, cavernous wood stoves going.

"The boys were real boys then as now, and some of their antics consisted of carrying fence gates to the depot platform, stealing horse blocks, digging up hitching posts, tick-tacking on church windows at nighttime, climbing to the roof of the old school building, or into the Methodist Church tower and ringing the bells, a sternly forbidden pastime。

"There was a fair ball field on the vacant pasture just east of Lake Avenue and 6th Street, and on Saturday afternoons or holidays our town boys entertained the entire populace in baseball combats with the neighboring town nines, and no league game of the present days excited more intense interest. The lake was the drawing point in summertime, and many the boy who played 'hooky' for an afternoon's forbidden swim."

With the election of Village officers and the completion of a sturdy, permanent brick railroad station, Wilmette had made its start as a suburban community. The next two decades of the 1880's and 1890's were to see a rapid growth both in population and business.

5

Growth in the 1880's and 1890's

GAGE'S ADDITION TO THE VILLAGE OF WILMETTE

Commercial Lith. Co. 123 Clark St.

LAKE MICHIGAN

MICHIGAN

MIDDLE LINE OF SECTION 27 & NORTH BOUNDARY OF WILMETTE VILLAGE

SEVENTH AVE.

| 9 | 8 | 7 | 6 | 27 | 5 | 4 | 3 |

SIXTH AVE.

GAGE   PARK   WILLIAM   WILMETTE   AVE.

| 10 | 11 | 12 | 13 |

FIFTH AVE.

| 17 | 16 | 15 | 14 |

FOURTH AVE.

| 22 | 18 | 19 | 20 | 21 |

NORTH LINE OF OUILMETTE RESERVATION AVE.

FOREST AVE.

ST.   ST.   ST.

LAKE AVE.

N
W   E
S

CENTRE AVE.

C. & N.W. R.R.

DEPOT

JOHN GAGE'S
Addition to Wilmette.

FOURTEEN MILES FROM CHICAGO COURT HOUSE.

Joins Evanston on the North.

THREE BLOCKS NORTH OF THE DEPOT AT WILMETTE,

Beginning on the East side of the Railroad and running through to the Lake, with a half mile of shore bluff thirty-three feet high. The beach here curves to the North, furnishing a beautiful and uninterrupted view all the way to Waukegan. Nearly all the shipping to and from Chicago is seen from this point.

SEVEN PASSENGER TRAINS

each way daily, stop at this Station.

COMMUTATION FARE ELEVEN CTS.

SOIL, a rich sandy loam ; mostly covered with a great variety of large and beautiful native forest trees.

FINE AVENUES, eighty feet wide, well graded and gravelled.

LOTS ARE LARGE, containing about six ordinary sized lots, and every lot is provided with perfect drainage.

SPECIAL INDUCEMENTS to parties who will build good houses.

Further information given and sales made by

ASAHEL GAGE,
HENRY H. GAGE, and
AUGUSTUS N. GAGE,
Room 14, Portland Block, Chicago,
Or by   JOHN GAGE,
Vineland, New Jersey.

MAP SHOWING LOCATION
OF
WILMETTE

Depot

Residence of Edwin Drury

Residence of Asahel Gage

Residence of Augustus N. Gage

Residence of Horace G. Drury

The decades of the 1880's and 1890's saw Wilmette transformed from a scattered settlement of houses, surrounded by thick woods and huddled within a few blocks of the depot, to a rapidly growing Chicago suburb. During these 20 years, the village residents would establish basic organizations from social clubs to schools, to meet the needs of the community. As the second decade closed the people of Wilmette would see the coming of Wilmette's second railroad.

In September, 1887, as Mrs. Lorin A. Bower (Esther Dunshee) recalled 60 years later, there were about "700 people in Wilmette. . . and the business of the village was done on West Railroad Avenue (now Green Bay Road) just opposite the North Western Station."

In that year, Max Mueller bought the two-year-old building on the northwest corner of that street and Wilmette Avenue and opened a general store, stocking boots, shoes, grain, groceries, notions and seed. His competitor was William H. Kinney's grocery across from the depot, which also housed the post office in a small side room, with a few postal boxes for patrons. In this bustling business section, there occurred Wilmette's first train fatalities, when, on Christmas Eve, the station agent, his wife, and their young son who lived in a cottage where the Central Hotel now stands were killed on a blizzardy night by a southbound train as they were returning from festivities at the Methodist church.

The real estate boom had begun, and realty agents like E. T. Paul lauded the beauties of Wilmette as "The

Gage's Addition Advertisement, Circa 1875. Gage family residences are shown, as well as homes of the Drury brothers. All four residences shown are today in their original locations, some remodeled considerably from their original exterior. Depot was relocated in the 1890's and again in 1974.

Elm Forest of the North," showing choice land sites to prospects from Chicago from a horse and buggy. Chicago was still the place where most of the residents worked, but news about the northern suburbs was spreading and families were coming up to house-hunt or to buy lots and build far from the city's pavements.

In December, 1880, 50 residents formed a literary society, paying a $1 initiation fee, and on May 4, 1882, the society was incorporated under Illinois law as the Wilmette Library Association, whose five directors were Frank L. Joy, Milton C. Springer, O. P. Gothlin, W. M. Wood, and Mrs. I. A. Thrasher. In February, 1889, Mrs. M. E. Barker organized the Library and Social Club and, as president, enrolled 23 young residents at the first meeting. The few books donated were kept in the Methodist church, and meetings were held in the homes of members. Three years later, the club's name was changed to the Elmwood Library Association and a charter was issued by the Illinois Secretary of State, providing for a circulating library.

Now a full-fledged library under state law, the Association rented Arcanum Hall (on the site of Lyman-Sargent's drug store) for a three-year period, to serve the 100 members. With characteristic initiative, W. E. Dibble raised $53 himself towards repairs on the hall, then furnished $200 in books, agreeing to repayment of $10 a month by the library. After a fire in 1895 damaged the books, John Panushka offered to house the books in a small room back of his office on Central Avenue, and to be librarian for $5 a month. But the location proved to be a poor one and books were not circulating, until the Woman's Club in 1897 rented rooms over a store on Central Avenue and paid members to work as librarians.

Max E. Mueller's Grocery Store, Circa 1893-94. Located on the northwest corner of Wilmette Avenue and Green Bay Road, the store photograph pictures, from left, August Butzow, Henry Schultz, Max E. Mueller, and daughter Clara seated on the wheeled cart.

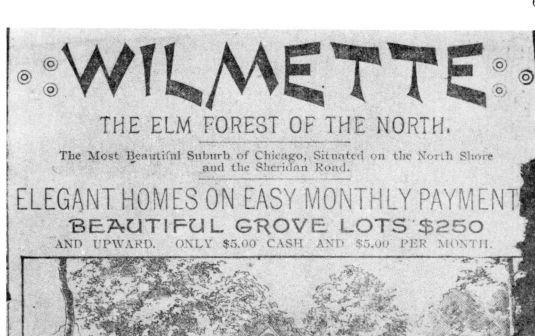

WILMETTE

THE ELM FOREST OF THE NORTH.

The Most Beautiful Suburb of Chicago, Situated on the North Shore and the Sheridan Road.

ELEGANT HOMES ON EASY MONTHLY PAYMENT
BEAUTIFUL GROVE LOTS $250
AND UPWARD. ONLY $5.00 CASH AND $5.00 PER MONTH.

A VIEW ON OUR SUBDIVISION.

Have you ever stopped to reflect that every dollar paid to us in Monthly Payments tow a home is so much **SAVED?**

The money you are paying to your landlord **IS GONE.**

The money paid to us is BUYING YOU A HOME, which you will own in a few years' will then be worth DOUBLE WHAT IT IS NOW.

All lots covered with Beautiful Forest Trees, are 171 feet deep; with building restrict such as will warrant a fine class of improvements.

WE HAVE ONLY A FEW LOTS LEFT

In this, our fourth, subdivision. BUY NOW, BEFORE PRICES ARE ADVANCED. A NORTH SHORE DEALERS HAVE ADVANCED THEIR PRICES EXCEPT US. Wilmette has a population of about 1,600 people, and is situated on the Lake Shore immediately adjoin ing the aristocratic suburb of Evanston, with its fine schools and churches, and is only 33 minutes' ride from Wells-st. Depot, and has 42 trains a day on the C. & N. W. Ry. Let us show you this property before you make your purchases in any of the prairie suburbs. TO SEE MEANS TO BUY.

Call at our office for FREE TICKETS for following Trains: Week days—11 a. m., 1 p. m., 2:20 p. m. Office open Sunday mornings from 9:30 to 10:30. Call and get tickets for our 11 o'clock train.

E. T. PAUL & CO., Main Floor, 116 LaSalle Street.

Real Estate Promotion in 1880. "The Most Beautiful Suburb" offered wooded lots as low as $250, and enticed prospective buyers with the location "adjoining the aristocratic suburb of Evanston" and 33-minute train ride from the Chicago depot. E. T. Paul himself was a village resident, living at Central and West (now Park) Avenues.

During the early 1890's, Wilmette women took an important step which through the intervening 85 years has had an important effect upon the community. In November, 1891, 20 women met in the home of the Misses Ida and Anna Law (the house still stands near the southeast corner of Forest and Twelfth Street) to organize the Woman's Club of Wilmette. Mrs. Herbert G. Leonard, the bride of the Methodist minister, was elected president. Three years later, the Club unsuccessfully petitioned the village board to install a drinking fountain designed for both humans and horses. Undismayed by the board's initial refusal, the ladies took the project into their own hands, placing an ornate iron fountain with two faucets at the intersection of Wilmette and Central Avenues.

Club members took turns reading books and original papers once a month, following the charter's objectives of "reading and discussing history, literature and art to promote. . . the moral, intellectual and social culture of its members." In 1893, club members visited the Columbian Exposition and, in May, attended the daily sessions of the Exposition's Congress of Women.

Wilmette was indeed growing. Lillian C. Brown recalled, in a 1931 article in the *Woman's Club Bulletin*, that in 1892 real estate agent Edwin Drury drove the Brown family in a carriage to look at homes, and that "before the afternoon was over we had leased, for eighteen dollars a month, an eight-room house with about three hundred feet of ground and fine trees." She recalled that the house had no plumbing and lighting was by kerosene lamps ("a hardship after city life"), but that gas pipes and water mains were already being laid, and that a further mark of civilization were the bathrooms being installed in homes by Gus (August) Specht, the village plumber who lived at the southeast corner of Lake Avenue and Tenth Street. Her

description of people and places in the '90's is well worth repeating in part:

"The simple homes had large grounds and all about was native forest where in springtime wild flowers grew in profusion. The favorite trail to the lake started at Elmwood Avenue and Tenth Street, rambled through lovely thick woods and came out at the big Gage home on Sheridan Road and Chestnut. Lake Avenue was cut through making it possible to go to the lake with horse and buggy. . . The public buildings in Wilmette were the school house, the town hall, the Methodist and Congregational churches and the Assembly Hall. . . used for public meetings and entertainments. . . . The outstanding out-of-door diversion was bicycling. . . On summer evenings young people and older people, too, would go out after an early dinner on single wheels or tandems for a spin along Sheridan Road to Evanston or to Glencoe and back. . . Picnics on the beach were popular. . . Sometimes family groups, sometimes parties of young people, would get together for a campfire supper preceded by a swim and followed by a sing. There were no bathhouses, so we dressed one at a time in a guarded tent improvised by draping blankets over bushes. We felt that our bathing suits like our bicycle outfits were the last word in freedom and modernity. They were of blue serge trimmed with white braid, made with bloomers, knee length skirt and elbow sleeves. If there were gentlemen in the party, we wore long black stockings. We did not make noteworthy swimming records."

Mechanical and technological progress was also a characteristic of Wilmette's 1890's decade. In the winter of 1892, residents forgot the chill of February when a

Overleaf.   Map of Wilmette by Real Estate Agents Spencer and McCadden, Circa 1891. At this time, our present Sheridan Road was called State Street. (Courtesy David C. Leach, Jr.)

toll station — a pioneer pay telephone — was installed in Max Mueller's store. Within a year or two, residents and businessmen were acquiring their own telephones and the telephone company decided to serve Wilmette subscribers from the Evanston exchange rather than establish one in the village, as rumors that Evanston would soon annex Wilmette circulated in late 1893 and early 1894. But Wilmette voted against annexation (see below) and in July, 1897, after the village board had modified the ordinance to clear the way, a local exchange was established in the back of druggist Samuel C. Sexauer's store, with twenty-eight customers and four miles of telephone pole lines. The next year, 27 new subscribers and a line to Kenilworth were added. By 1899, Wilmette could count 92 telephone subscribers, and the system added automatic signaling equipment for party line users.

During the early 1890's, many of the 1,500 Wilmette residents took active sides in the proposal that the village be annexed to Evanston. Those for annexation called themselves the Annexation Club, while residents who opposed annexation to their neighbor to the south formed a group called the Wilmette Citizens Association. The full story would require more space than this book can allow, but the issue caused tempers to flare up and both sides to issue circulars and letters with facts and figures, not to mention a little impassioned oratory. Briefly, the main arguments centered about the question of sending Wilmette children to Evanston High School, and the financial need to become a part of Evanston.

The Annexation Club, led by E. A. Burge, Louis J. Pierson, Benjamin F. Hill, Sr., Horace G. Drury, and Father William Netstraeter, argued that annexation would bring major benefits to the people of Wilmette, including more support for the high school (New Trier Township High School was not to be opened for almost seven years), lower real estate taxes, electric street lights, better fire and police protection, a share in the ownership of Evanston's water plant, and, as one circular promised, all the advantages of "the progressive, educational and moral forces of the splendid city of Evanston." Those who supported the Wilmette Citizens Association argued that Wilmette was indeed financially strong and could expect a bright future independently; that annexation would not change the right of the children to attend the high school; and that the village would realize its greatest potential by remaining independent. In the winter of 1894, the campaign reached its hottest heights. At a January 23 Library Hall meeting, which the press called "full of tobacco smoke, full of people and of hard feelings," Judge Augustus Gage, a leading opponent of annexation, was accused by the meeting chairman R. Boddinghouse of "playing the fool," and the judge, a large man, walked menacingly to the front. Both sides spoke, and the circulars continued their rounds. Walter E. Dibble addressed one to his "Fellow Citizens," urging them to oppose annexation because "we have the handsomest and best located village of its size on all the shores of Lake Michigan. . . and all we need is the same rapid rate of progress. . . to make our village a veritable paradise." On April 10, a special referendum on the annexation issue was held. Annexation was defeated by three votes. A week later, Evanston voters turned out a heavy vote, supporting annexation by 735 to 596. That fall, a new Wilmette referendum was held. But this time, 162 votes opposed it, and 138 supported it. Wilmette's vote decided the

MAP OF **WILMETTE**

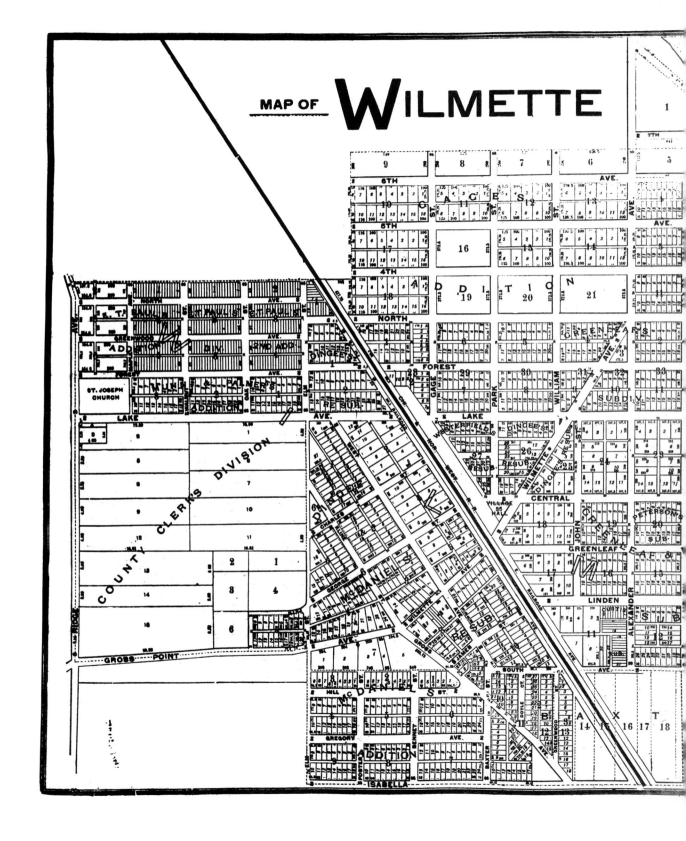

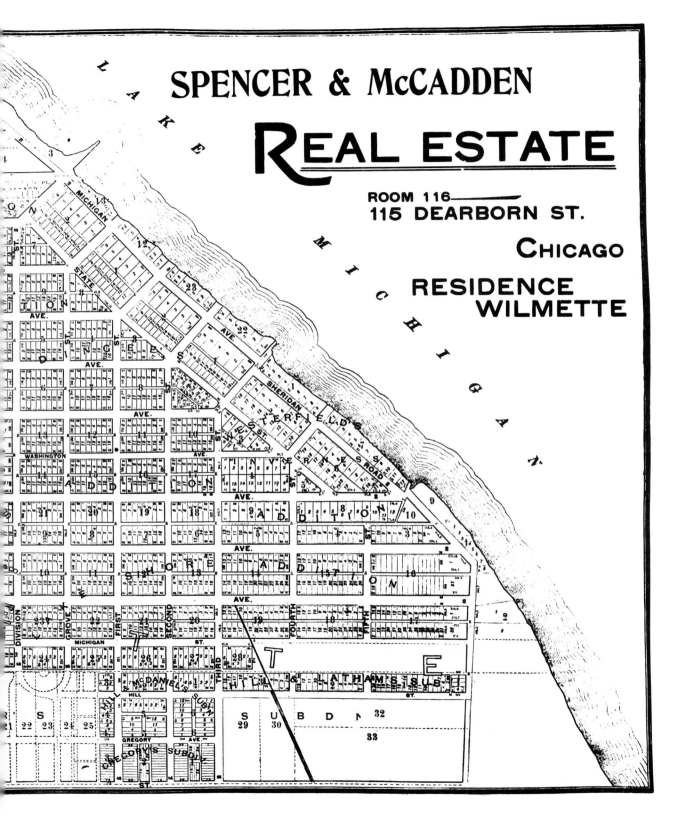

SPENCER & McCADDEN

REAL ESTATE

ROOM 116
115 DEARBORN ST.

CHICAGO

RESIDENCE WILMETTE

issue, and the citizens cast their lot with a continuing independence.

Paralleling the coming of the telephone to Wilmette in the 1890's, railroad transportation serving the village also expanded, first, and briefly, by steam, then by electric power. In 1894, the Chicago, Milwaukee and St. Paul extended its steam line from Chicago through Evanston to a station at the northwest corner of Third Street and Maple Avenue, an area called Llewellyn Park. In the 1870's, the area was called Hillville, for the pioneer Hill family, Arunah, who settled in 1837, and his son Benjamin Franklin Hill, who built several of the first Wilmette houses in this section, and owned much of the land near the railroad terminal.

America's crowded cities were clamoring for interurban transportation during the 1890's, and the new electric street railway provided the answer. In 1894, in Waukegan, the Bluff City Electric Street Railway, recalling that city's original name, was being constructed from Waukegan as far as the North Chicago city limits. Four years later, the electric railway had pushed south to Highland Park, and by 1899, was running to Wilmette's Llewellyn Park, to connect with the C. M & St.P. trains to Chicago.

In 1899, the Bluff City railroad had laid its tracks east of the North Western (now the bicycle path from Kenilworth to downtown Wilmette) through Wilmette. From its north and southbound stations (on the present site of the International House of Pancakes and its parking lot), the route turned sharply east, then ran in the middle of Greenleaf Avenue to Fourth Street, making a wide curve across a field to its Linden Avenue station. In August, 1899, the railroad began service into Evanston. Train service along Greenleaf Avenue was

never accepted by many residents, who often protested the operation to the village board, but Wilmette needed the transportation for its growing population, and took no official action.

The decade of the 1890's also saw the growth of the Wilmette school system. Education was a major concern of the citizens, and one of the earliest institutions in the area was the first one-room log schoolhouse built by William Foster in 1839 or 1840, at his cooperage on the present 1827 Wilmette Avenue location. Foster's daughter, Martha, was the teacher for the three younger Foster children and for seven other neighbor children, one of whom was James Mulligan,

Interiors of Wilmette Home of the 1890's. These unidentified photographs provide a glimpse of the decor and furnishings of a typical home of the period, from the hanging kerosene lamp, halltree and patterned carpet to the piano covered with an ornamental shawl and coal-burning fireplace.

Wilmette Woman of the 1890's. This unidentified young woman is wearing the long skirt, high-neck blouse and tie, and large hat of the period, and may have been a student or teacher.

later to organize Mulligan's Raiders in the Civil War. About this time, a log school was built east of Sheridan Road and north of Canterbury Court (a plaque commemorates the school at the entrance to that street).

The log schoolhouse stood near the graves of several Indians, and an early teacher, Mrs. Harriet M. Anderson, many years later remembered seeing sailing schooners pass by on the lake so close that she could read the names.

In 1846, Bartholomew Hoffmann opened a school in the Gross Point area for five students, and classes were taught in the kitchen by his son, Franz Joseph (see Chapter III). As more families settled in Wilmette, a frame schoolhouse was built in 1863 to replace the Foster cabin on Wilmette Avenue, to educate 22 students. Annie Gertrude Gedney, who was about ten years old when the school opened, recalled many years later that as a student she used slates and pens, wrote in the Spencerian style, and read from an early *McGuffey Reader*. Among the fellow students, Annie Gedney (later Mrs. Edward Mendsen) remembered, were James D. Kline, (father of early Wilmette historian James D. W. Kline), George McDaniel (son of Alexander McDaniel), and Frank and Mame Westerfield (children of John Gedney Westerfield). It is interesting to note that Evanston opened its first school in 1845, Glencoe in 1856, and Winnetka in 1859. They were all primarily private schools, and taught very small classes of children in the immediate vicinity.

Wilmette's first public school opened in the fall of 1871, on a half acre of land donated for one dollar by Mr. and Mrs. Henry A. Dingee at the corner of Tenth Street and Central Avenue. It was a one-room building, and Mary Sheldon was the first teacher, serving until

Wilmette Office of E. T. Paul Real Estate Company, Circa 1894. Large sign in this faded photograph promises "modern" houses, low prices and "easy monthly payments," as well as houses for rent and vacant lots for sale "in all parts of Wilmette." Photograph donated by Mrs. Brook Ballard, originally in the possession of her husband's aunt.

1890 Advertisement. Accompanied map of the young community.

DRURY BROTHERS,
Real Estate.

NORTH LAKE SHORE A SPECIALTY.

Choice Residence Sites for Sale in Wilmette,

Also a few First Class Lots Suitable for business locations and a limited number of Dwellings. You will find this property PRECISELY AS REPRESENTED, 30 feet above Lake Michigan, Fine Soil, Beautiful Native Elms and other trees. A most Decided Bargain at our prices. **TITLE PERFECT.**

Saloons forever prohibited by State Law.

CHICAGO OFFICE. 1110 TACOMA BUILDING
And Residents of Wilmette for past SEVENTEEN Years.

Bluff City Electric Railway Company Train, Circa 1898. The track crew poses with shovels in front of Car No. 4. The second photograph, taken about the same time, is a side view of a train carrying passengers. Locations are unknown.

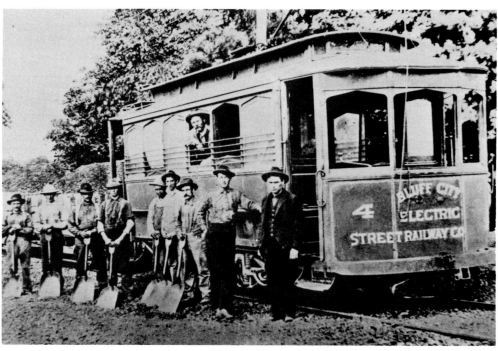

1892. Alice Wheelock remembered many years later that "the graveled school grounds were devoid of any kind of play equipment, and the only visible item was an iron pump with a tin cup. . . children were summoned to school by a hand bell rung vigorously by the janitor. . ." In addition to the three R's, students studied history, geography, art, and music. This first school district served the area east of the tracks and west to Fifteenth Street. To meet the growth of the school-age population, two wings were added with a tower, and the entrance was moved from Central to the Tenth Street side.

Illinois in 1883 passed the state's first compulsory education laws, which changed the practice of many parents of sending their children to school long enough to learn to read and write, then keeping them at home to help. In 1891, the original wood frame Central School building was razed and an eight-classroom brick building was built in 1892, on land purchased in 1889 from the Dingees. A. J. Lyon was appointed principal. There was no high school in New Trier Township, so Wilmette children who were graduated from grade school went to Evanston until 1901 when New Trier High School opened. In 1896, Wilmette's first kindergarten was started, with Clara H. Uecke as the first teacher. By the fall of 1894, Central School students could take high school courses from Latin and mythology to history and mathematics, and enter high school with advanced standing.

Wilmette's second school was named after Civil War General John A. Logan, and was built in 1893 as a wooden one-room building on Kline Street (now Prairie Avenue) for the first and second grades. Two years later, a two-room brick schoolhouse was built for Gross Point on Wilmette Avenue, just west of Ridge Avenue (now the Peter J. Huerter American Legion Post), to serve that community's 61 students. By 1896, Wilmette schools had an enrollment of 325 and five full-time teachers and their first superintendent, Alfred E. Logie.

A growing village created the need for protection from fire which could quickly destroy the wooden houses and businesses of that time. In 1894, Wilmette bought two hose carts and organized two volunteer fire groups, one to serve the east side, the other the area west of the railroad tracks at Green Bay Road. Fire Company No. 1 was stationed at 1035 Lake Avenue and used the Methodist church bell as an alarm signal. Company No. 2 was quartered in the J. B. Spencer barn in Vattman Park, installing a school bell for its alarm. Together, the two fire companies had a force of 40 men, all volunteers.

In 1899, Wilmette built its first central fire station on the site of the present post office, facing Central Avenue, with a high tower used to dry 50-foot lengths of hoses and as a fire watch. In April, 1906, Walter H. Zibble, later to become fire marshal, was the driver and lived with his family on the second floor.

By the mid-1890's, Wilmette's 1873 Chicago and North Western railroad depot was obsolete for the commuters to and from Chicago. The pioneer station had no water or electricity, and no adequate waiting room facilities. In 1896, the Chicago and North Western agreed to build a larger station on the east side of the tracks and by 1897, the station was serving the Wilmette commuters and shoppers. Late in 1975, this depot was torn down when the new Village Hall was built and expanded to the west.

Original Central School, After 1871. Built in 1871 as a one-room school, on land at Tenth and Central donated by the Henry Dingees, Central School later was expanded with the additions of a tower and two wings, as shown here. In 1891, a brick eight-classroom building replaced this wooden structure, as the population of schoolchildren grew.

First Logan School, on Kline Street, Circa 1900. Originally a one-room building built in 1893 on present-day Prairie Avenue, Logan was enlarged by adding two rooms and an entrance hall, as shown in this photograph. When the second school was erected in 1911, the building was used as a manual training center for the Wilmette district until destroyed by fire in March, 1916.

74

First Grade Class at Central School, 1895. Photograph was taken on the front porch steps of the Tuttle house, adjacent to the school. One boy holds a miniature derby hat, and both boys and girls wear high button shoes of the period.

Advertisements, 1898. 440 Kline Street was at the southeast corner of Kline and Grosse Point Rd., now Prairie and Wilmette.

Wilmette's First Dairy.
In this late 1890's
photograph, a milkman who
may be Walter H. Zibble,
prepares to leave for a
delivery from the dairy
barns, located on the Peter
M. Hoffman farm on west
Lake Avenue. Customers
had a choice of one of two
deliveries a day, at 2 a.m.
and in the afternoon. In
1902, Witt moved the
dairy to 718 Twelfth
Street, and in 1907, sold
his business to the Bowman
Dairy Company.

Pioneer Real Estate Developer Edgar T. Paul. A native of Toronto, Canada, Paul served as Village president from 1892-1893, and reported to the Trustees that during his year he built "over 100 mud crossings. . . at a cost of about $1,000."

Edwin Drury House, May, 1880. One of four homes in the Gage advertisement, the house remains today at 1112 Greenwood Avenue. Edwin's brother Horace Greeley Drury served as Village president from 1895 to 1897, after two years as a trustee, and as a park commissioner from 1908 until his death in 1922. After learning the building trade in Chicago, the brothers moved to Wilmette in 1873, and built many early homes, later entering the real estate business.

Wilmette's First Fire Equipment. One of two horse-drawn hose carts purchased in 1894 for the east and west side volunteer fire companies, and the only equipment used until the first horse-drawn fire wagon was added in 1905. The young firefighter is Albert Zibble, son of Walter H. Zibble, the department's paid driver.

Wilmette Sunday Evening Supper Club, 1890's. Tams were all the rage for the young ladies, two of whom hold books, perhaps for reading aloud to the group. Young men are somewhat outnumbered by the gentle sex.

Advertisements, 1898.

G. J. HAPP

PRACTICAL

HORSE SHOER and

Blacksmith

SATISFACTION GUARANTEED

Telephone 1641

1234 Central Ave.   -   Wilmette, Ill.

F. J. Van Order & Son

Can supply your wants in
up-to-date LIVERY

. . Good Surreys and Horses . .

••••••••

Baggage and Expressing

Phone No. 9 and we will come

Interior of Hoffmann Brothers Grocery, 1890's. Phillip and John A. Hoffmann started both a general store and a coal, wood and lumber yard in 1888, in a frame building at Ridge and Wilmette Avenues, replaced in 1901 by a larger brick and stone store building destroyed by fire in December, 1909. Note the spotless floor and order baskets behind the woman customer.

80

By 1890, Wilmette had a population of almost 1,500, and clearly needed an official Village Hall. A two-story building with arched front portico, bay windows and balcony with flag pole was completed that year, on the triangle of land now occupied by the 1976 Village Hall. Twenty years later, the building was inadequate, and plans were made for a new, larger facility.

By the turn of the century, Wilmette had established the basic institutions and organization for growth. In 60 years, the village had evolved from a few scattered houses in the woods to a community of more than 2,000 people, with still more growth to come in the next few decades.

Path thro' woods.
M. F.
Butternut Hunt

Gathering Butternuts, late 1890's. Young lady on woodland path is well prepared with basket and flowered hat to shield the overhead sun's rays. Location is unknown.

6

Religion Sheds Its Light

Wilmette's growth and progress have been and continue to be directly related to the diversity and strength of its churches. Here, as everywhere in the nation, religion was an important part of family life. In the first decades before the competition of the automobile, radio, and rapid public transportation, the churches were the center of social and civic life for the citizens of the Village.

Interestingly, in a community which became heavily Protestant, the first religion was Roman Catholic. The groundwork was laid by Antoine Ouilmette, when he helped establish St. Mary's Church in Chicago in 1833, a few years after he left Chicago's Fort Dearborn settlement to live in his log cabin on the lake. Ten years later, the German Catholic farmers who settled on the western edge of Wilmette founded St. Joseph's Church in a small log cabin (see Chapter III) on the northwest corner of Ridge and Lake Avenues, near the site of the present church cemetery.

In 1849, a frame church was completed, to be replaced in 1869 by a large brick church, under the leadership of Father William Netstraeter. In 1939, the present St. Joseph's Church, built in Romanesque style, opened for parish worship on the southeast corner of Ridge and Lake Avenues.

By 1900, Catholic families whose members did not speak German were moving into east Wilmette. Late in June, 1904, St. Francis Xavier Church was founded for families who had traveled a considerable distance to St. Mary's Church in central Evanston before the coming of the elevated or the automobile. Mass was first held in the new church on Christmas Day, 1905, and the first pastor was Father Edward Byrnes. Early in 1910, the parishioners built a parish school adjacent to the

St. Joseph's Church, Circa 1870. Church as shown in photograph replaced a frame structure in 1869, and, in turn, was replaced in 1939 by the present church on Ridge and Lake Avenues. School is left, parish house on right. (Courtesy Marion Hoffmann)

church. In 1937, Reverend Martin D. McNamara became the fifth pastor of St. Francis Xavier and in February, 1939, the present gothic-style church was completed.

Wilmette was still two years away from becoming an incorporated village when, on December 1, 1870, a group of Protestant sects met and formed a committee to raise funds for a church to serve the co-operative Wilmette Evangelical Association. Donations were made by Baptists, Methodists, Congregationalists, Presbyterians, and Episcopalians, and real estate operator Luther L. Greenleaf donated the lots for the church. The undated list of donors includes the names of Wilmette's leading land developers and village fathers, including Greenleaf, John G. Westerfield, Henry Dingee, Jared Gage, E. R. and C. D. Paul, and Alexander McDaniel, each listed with the amount of his subscription and his religious denomination.

St. Francis Xavier Church, Circa 1905. St. Francis was established in 1904 as a second Catholic parish at Ninth and Linden to serve the non-German Catholics who did not belong to St. Joseph's on Ridge Road, and had traveled to attend St. Mary's Church in Evanston.

Wilmette Evangelical Association Subscription List, 1873. List followed an agreement to establish the Association and deed of lots by real estate businessman Luther I. Greenleaf in July, 1873. Money was used to build church at Lake Avenue and Wilmette Avenues, and included Greenleaf, Henry A. Dingee, Alexander McDaniel, Absalom Gedney and other pioneer leaders. The reverse of the agreement is shown on the following page.

	Name.	For what denomination.	Amount.
Feb 24 paid $100	L. L. Greenleaf	Congregational	$450.00
Nov 15 paid $25	C. D. Paul	Protestant Episcopal	125.00
July paid $100	Isaac R. Kirk & wm Paul	Methodist Episcopal	125.00
April 18 1873 Paid July 50	N. Paul	Congregational	125.00
Paid July 29/73 $250	C. H. Moore ⅌ L. L. Greenleaf	Congregational	250.00
Paid 66 Aug 9 /73	Dawson Kemp	Methodist Episcopal	100.00
Oct 25/73 Paid in full	E. R. Paul	Baptist	100.00
Aug 4 paid $870.75		Baptist	625.00
	Henry A. Dinger	Protestant Episcopal	450.00
Paid $800.00	Wm Daniel	Methodist	800.00
Paid $100	G Westerfield	Baptist	100.00
	Seb. Kline		100.00
July 31 paid $50 Oct 2 paid 15	Obadiah Huse	Methodist	200.00
Methodist	John H Foster	paid $50	50.00
Paid $50	John Culver	Methodist	50.00
Paid $10	Jared Gage	Methodist	10.00
Paid $10	John Daig		10.00
Paid 10	Charles McDaniel		10.00
Paid $25.00	Henry Conts	Protestant Episcopal	25.00
x	C P Rothfull	Baptist	20.00
x	L Hittend	"	20.00
Paid by Credit	Nich Smith	"	15.00
Paid by hauling Gravel	Lar Mahon	"	10.00

Paid by Store pk Ck	A. J. Sherman	Cong Baptist	15.00
Paid July 24/71	C. L. Greenleaf	Baptist	
Paid $10 aug 7 pd 10	Mrs. Wm Dwyer	Methodist	20 Paid
paid 10 aug 7 pd 10	Mr. S. M. Dwyer	Do	20 Paid
aug 6 paid $10	C. A. Vail	Presbyterian	10 paid
Paid oct 9/71	M. A. Gedney	Methodist	10.00
paid $7	Mrs. A. L. Glidden	Baptist	10.00
	John Sherman		5.00
paid $25	Lambert Blum	Methodist	25 paid
paid $200	A. McDaniel	Methodist	200.00
Nov 3 paid $10		Congregational	
paid $25 Sept 23	Lambert Blum	paid in brick, Methodist	25.00
paid $25	Henry Curley	Protestant Episcopal	25.00
Paid By Note			
paid Sept 17 $25			25.00
	Henry A. Singer	Baptist	200.00
Non paid 5	200 Paid		
" 10			
" 100			
oct paid $25	J. V. Kline		$25.00
oct 25 Paid $13	A. J. Jordan & Co	2 Kegs 3d Nails	13.00
paid $27.10	North Western R R Com., Refunded 1/3 of Freight Money on Lumber		27.10
	J. J. Webster	Baptist	

Particularly interesting are several entries of non-money gifts, such as the installation of a lightning rod and building cornices, and two kegs of nails. The Chicago and North Western Railway contributed too, submitting a bill for transporting lumber of $27.10, one-third the regular rate. Church services were conducted by Evanston divinity professors, Garrett Biblical Institute students, or by Dr. E. N. Packard, pastor of Evanston's Congregational Church. The Association quietly disappeared (as was probably intended) as each denomination moved to organize its own church.

In the fall of 1873, a year after Wilmette became a Village, Methodists led by Mr. and Mrs. Milton C. Springer began to worship in the new frame Central School building at Central Avenue and Tenth Street. At first, in 1875 and 1876, the 23-member congregation rented a frame church built on the northeast corner of Lake and Wilmette Avenues by Henry Dingee.

Fire alarms as well as the deaths of neighbors were announced to the little community by the tolling of the church bell, now displayed in the church park on the west side of Wilmette Avenue. For his hours of dedicated service, the pastor, who changed churches on a rotation basis, received $350 a year, and for this salary, he also served as a counselor and taught school.

After several years, the Methodists bought the building, holding services there until the spring of 1908, when a growing 247-member congregation made necessary the building of a larger brick church. Ground was broken in October, and on June 13, 1909, the church opened for worship by its members, with music from a pipe organ for which Andrew Carnegie contributed a philanthropic $900. In September, 1928,

after the brick church and two adjoining houses were razed, the cornerstone for the present church was laid, and the following June the sanctuary was dedicated.

Wilmette's Congregational Church was born June 3, 1875, in the historic home of Andrew Taylor Sherman, where three years earlier the Village was formed and John G. Westerfield was elected the first president. In 1876, the Rev. Edward P. Wheeler of Beloit was chosen to be the first pastor. For eight years, services were held in the one-story frame Central School, whose child-sized desks must have cramped the bodies if not the style of church members.

By 1882, the 60 members began to raise money to build a frame church on Eleventh Street, a half-block south of Lake Avenue opposite the present church school playground. The church was dedicated in September, 1883, and was again replaced by the present church building, which began services on January 1, 1905, and was built on land donated by Mrs. Mary E. Gates. In the fall of 1909, the auditorium and basement rooms were completed and the church looked much as it does today.

There is still a vestige of the frame church, which today serves as the garage for the house at 738 Eleventh Street, with its telltale arched gothic windows, long boarded up. In 1920, the congregation bought land for a playground south of the church, with a 175-foot frontage on both Wilmette Avenue and Eleventh Street. The south portion of the lot is the site for housing for the elderly still to be built as this book is being completed.

As early as 1871, Episcopal prayer services were being held alternately in the Wilmette homes of Thomas B. Morris and John Stevenson. For a time, services were

held on the second floor of Arcanum Hall, and a Sunday school started. In September, 1893, the congregation celebrated its first Holy Communion, and in October, the mission was named St. Augustine's and formally organized the following year, with a finance committee to purchase land and plan a church. Ground was broken for the church February 28, 1898, and the cornerstone laid April 3. The church opened for worship July 10, 1898, the day designated by President William McKinley for national thanksgiving for the victory of the navy at Santiago during the Spanish-American War.

In March, 1910, the parish was organized and admitted to the Diocese of Chicago, and the large congregation began to plan a larger church structure on land adjoining the original building. By Christmas, 1911, the new church building was open for services, the original church becoming the parish house. In October, 1942, the parish house structure was being razed when a fire seriously damaged the church, and services were held for ten weeks in the old First National Bank on Wilmette Avenue, followed by Christmas services in the

Wilmette's First Methodist Church, 1906. Rented starting in 1875, the frame building was built by Henry Dingee. In 1908, the building was replaced by a red brick church, which, in turn, was replaced in 1928 by the present structure at Lake and Wilmette Avenues. Photo above shows interior decorated for Christmas. The congregation adopted the name Trinity Church of the North Shore in the late 1960's.

Wilmette Methodist Church. A month later, services were held in the restored church, with a special sermon by Bishop Frank E. Wilson, pastor of the church for several years before World War I.

Wilmette Presbyterians began services in August, 1911, in the Woman's Club, with 40 families, and the following November, a building committee was organized to plan a church structure. Dr. James M. Wilson was installed as pastor in December, and construction began July 23, 1912, with the cornerstone laying in September. The church was dedicated May 25, 1913, and the chapel structure opened to serve the 200 members. For a week in October, 1918, the church was closed because of the national influenza epidemic. After a temporary frame building was completed for Sunday school classes in late 1919, work began on a larger church building in 1923 and 1924, and a three-story extension was added to the chapel.

On December 19, 1929, during bitter weather and a heavy blizzard, the church was entirely destroyed by fire. Despite the Depression conditions, plans for a third church were begun and by September, 1933, the new church held its first regular service. Three years later, a chapel seating 100 was completed and in August, 1944, the house at 826 Greenleaf Avenue was purchased and remodeled for a manse.

As early as 1893, Wilmette Lutherans were worshipping west of Green Bay Road, led by the Rev. J. D. Matthius, pastor of Bethlehem Lutheran Church of Evanston. On November 11, 1906, the first St. John's Lutheran Church was dedicated at Prairie and Linden Avenues, a wooden building with a belltower. Between 1910 and 1912 a parsonage was built. By 1920, the frame church was inadequate. The need for a larger

In the Interest of CHURCH GOING

Punctuality meets an engagement. Promptness meets a situation. But procrastination meets neither. "Tomorrow" is the eighth day of the week—when idlers work and some folks plan to begin church-going.

First Congregational Church
Sunday Morning at Eleven

Newspaper Advertisement, 1920.

First Congregational Church, Circa 1900. The first structure was built in 1883 on the east side of Eleventh Street and was in use until a new building was completed early in 1905 on the present site across the street.

St. Augustine's Episcopal Church, Circa 1911. Built in 1898 as St. Augustine's Mission, the church opened for worship July 10, 1898, the date designated by proclamation of President William McKinley as a day of national thanksgiving for the American naval victory at Santiago during the Spanish American War.

Cornerstone Ceremony, St. Augustine's Mission, 1898. The cornerstone was laid April 3, 1898, with suitable choir selections and prayer, and the church opened for services July 10.

church compelled the members to meet, determine that a new Lutheran Church was needed, and buy the land at Wilmette and Park Avenues in early June, 1921. The chapel was dedicated on January 7, 1923, and in December the members marched in procession to the new church. By 1933, St. John's served 370 communicants, and plans to add a parish hall were revived. In 1944, a lot east of the church was purchased, and the parish house was completed several years later.

Wilmette Christian Scientists who had been members of the First Church of Christ, Scientist, in Chicago, chartered their church on November 10, 1896, ten members strong. The following February, the Wilmette church was recognized as a branch of the Mother Church in Boston, and services were held until 1903 in a small store at 1152 Central Avenue. For the next three years, members met in a public hall, then at 1217 Wilmette Avenue.

In 1905, the original church building was constructed on the site of the present church at Tenth Street and Central Avenue. The first services were held in the completed structure May 13, 1906, and the church was formally dedicated September 24, 1911, when the building had been completely paid for. The church had a seating capacity of only 200, and in 1916 it was enlarged to double the capacity by raising the building to build a basement Sunday school room and by adding to the rear of the church. In 1915, a reading room was established several blocks west in the business district, and in 1935 located in the 1100 block of Central Avenue, where it remains today. In 1899, three years after the church was chartered, the first free Christian Science public lecture was given, and later, a series of lectures about Christian Science were held annually in the Village. Since 1941, there has been an annual outdoor lecture in the Bowl at Gillson Park.

The Rev. B. Frank Taber was the first pastor of the Wilmette Baptist Church, organized on April 6, 1913, with an initial membership of 62. Two years later, the membership had doubled and had purchased the present church site at Wilmette and Forest Avenues. By May, 1920, with a part of the funds raised, construction began on a new church building, designed by church member Howard Bowen. Members were using the basement for services in the fall of 1921, and the church structure was dedicated in April, 1924, with the total debt cleared in 1941. In 1970, the name was changed to Community Church of Wilmette.

St. John's Lutheran Church, circa 1906. Located at the northeast corner of Linden and Prairie Avenues, the building is now in use as a private home.

First Church of Christ, Scientist, Circa 1906. This picture shows the church before alterations enlarged the facilities in 1916. The present church replaced this one in 1962.

Wilmette's second Baptist church was founded much later as the Skokie Valley Baptist Church. The church was organized on October 2, 1952, with 85 charter members and met at Sharp Corner School in Skokie. Church members held property on Gross Point Road across from Sharp Corner School, but sold it and bought the land on the east side of Skokie Highway north of Lake Avenue, where the present church was built during 1959. The first services were held here in June, 1960, and the first full-time pastor was Arthur E. H. Barber. The present church membership is more than 400.

Wilmette's world-famous and much-photographed Baha'i Temple and the Baha'i faith had their beginnings when the village was chosen nearly 70 years ago as the center of the faith's North American movement. In April, 1908, the first purchase of land was made for a House of Worship, and on May 1, 1912, Baha'i's gathered at the northwest corner of Linden Avenue and Sheridan Road to break ground and to hear the dedication address of 'Abdu'l-Baha, son of the Baha'i founder and world leader.

By 1920, the design of the Temple by Wilmette resident Louis J. Bourgeois was approved, with its nine

96

**Old First Presbyterian
Church, Before 1924.** Gas
streetlight helps date the
photograph before
installation of electric
streetlights in 1924. Building
burned December 19, 1929
during severe blizzard.

The Cover, Wilmette Life, August 30, 1963. Advertising the 27th Annual Ice Cream Social at the Wilmette Parish Methodist Church are young people from the youth group portraying an era when ice cream socials first were popular: (from left, rear) Georgia Ference, Bill Robinson, Linda Coulthurst, Jack Confrey, and (seated) Harlene Edwards, Stephanie Ference and Marilyn Turner (courtesy Tri-Mu, Trinity Church).

Wilmette County Fair, 1904. Carnival and country fair combined, this event was sponsored by the Episcopal churchwomen, and was held on 13th Street, north of Lake Ave. Games, theatrics and box suppers were featured.

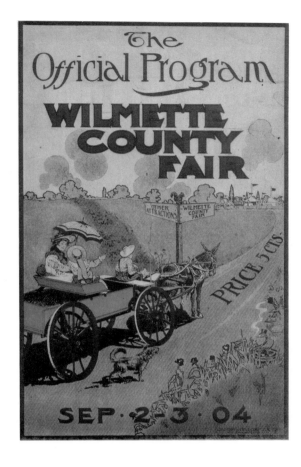

Skokie Valley Baptist Church, Under Construction, 1959. Interesting view of supporting A-frame beams as building frame is completed. Church, on Skokie Boulevard, was opened in 1960.

Wilmette Baptist Church, Before 1928. In 1970, the name was changed to Community Church of Wilmette. In 1913, Baptists organized and the building cornerstone was laid in 1920.

BAHA'I TEMPLE
Oct. 31, 1930

BAHA'I TEMPLE
Dec. 6, 1930
43

**Baha'i Temple Under
Construction, 1930.**
Internationally famous
and an outstanding
Wilmette visitor's attraction,
these photographs show an
early stage of construction in
October, 1930 (top) during
the erection of the steel work
for the main story, gallery
and clerestory, and (below)
steel dome construction
completed in December.
Bottom photo shows the
Temple as it appears today.
Purchase of the land was in
1908, and construction began
in December, 1920.

Church of Jesus Christ of Latter Day Saints, 1962. This Mormon Stake House was dedicated May 6, 1962, and followed the organization of the membership in 1936.

Wilmette Lutheran Church, 1962. Present building completed in 1929 is the second church building, replacing frame structure dedicated in 1906. (Courtesy Wilmette Life)

sides and unique use of architectural concrete. In December of that year, the foundation was built on nine supporting caissons resting on bedrock 124 feet below ground level. The steel and concrete superstructure was built between September, 1930, and April, 1931, and the interior work was begun in 1948. On May 2, 1953, the House of Worship was dedicated to public worship, with the landscaping of the grounds also completed.

Wilmette's Baha'i Temple is the second to be constructed, inspired by the original in the city of Ishqabad in southern Russia, built in the early 1890's.

As the western section of Wilmette began to develop into an area of new homes, the village population grew in the area which was once Gross Point farmland. In February, 1958, a number of young, conservative Jews met in Wilmette's Odd Fellows Hall to organize Beth Hillel Congregation. On April 16, Beth Hillel was formally chartered with 137 male members. Ground was broken for a religious school in 1961, a high priority for the young families. The sanctuary of the synagogue at 3220 Big Tree Lane, near Edens Expressway, was dedicated in June, 1971.

Unitarians are one of Wilmette's newest religious groups, having begun here as a fellowship group in 1964.

Meetings were held at Central School, and in 1967 the Lake Shore Unitarian Universalists called the Rev. Edgar C. Peara as minister. With a present membership of 200, the Unitarians now meet in the Wilmette Community Building.

Thus by Wilmette's centennial year of 1972, the Village population was about equally divided among these primary religious groups, each contributing in many ways to the strength and welfare of the community.

Beth Hillel Congregation. Completed in 1971, the synagogue and religious school now serve over 500 families.

7

The 20th Century Begins: 1900-1920

Decoration Day Parade, 1905. In this interesting sequence of three closely-spaced photographs, the parade's lead marchers, police with the large badges of the time, enter the intersection of Central Avenue and Wilmette Avenue, then the band passes with a band of small boys tagging along, and finally, the fire department with shouldered axes passes. Note the little girl on skates at lower right, and two women visiting at upper left. View is southeast from the drug store corner, with the McDaniel house in left background.

In 1900, Wilmette was a village of 2,300 people, with 12 trains daily each way, six miles of paving and a sewer and water system not yet connected to many homes. On July 23, 1901, 22-year-old Earl E. Orner arrived, to be the station agent for the Chicago and North Western Railway. Twenty-five years later, he recalled the Wilmette he found as a young man, a community where people came to the depot early to visit with neighbors before the train arrived, to whisk passengers to the Chicago terminal in 45 minutes. With his clerk, Henry Atkins, Orner opened the depot at 5:30 a.m. and closed the station at 7:30 p.m., seven days a week. William H. Egan and Frank M. Paul operated a flourishing horse cab business for railroad passengers, and for 50 cents their livery service rented open surreys. Cab drivers attired in brass-buttoned coats and plug hats collected the 15-cent fare, a bargain when the heavy rains made unpaved streets a quagmire, and the wooden sidewalks floated away or were appropriated as rafts by Wilmette boys.

Commercial businesses and public buildings grew in spurts. In 1902, philanthropist Andrew Carnegie offered to donate $10,000 towards building a free public library in Wilmette, if the village provided a suitable site and guaranteed $1,000 annually to maintain the library. To settle a controversy about locating the library east or west of the tracks, the directors submitted the question to public vote, and on January 2, 1905, the building was completed on the site of the present library, and opened to residents.

Wilmette Beach, North Towards Gage's Pier. Undated photograph shows rough bluffs and undeveloped beach area, and was probably taken shortly after 1900.

Wilmette Free Public Library, Circa 1905. Photograph was taken shortly after the library was completed, with $10,000 donated three years earlier by Andrew Carnegie.

Wilmette's Second Depot, Circa 1900. Photograph shows Village Hall at left. Carriage is probably livery service, forerunner of taxis, to meet passengers. Depot was razed in 1975, when new Village Hall was built, for parking area.

McGuire & Orr Real Estate Office, Circa 1903. Located on the northwest corner of Twelfth Street and Central Avenue, the building was later the site of the Wilmette Bank.

The Wilmette Directory for 1898 had listed 35 kinds of businesses from baggage express, bicycle repair and Mrs. L. H. Dalrymple's boarding house at 519 W. Railroad Avenue, to dentist C. H. Eldred, S. C. Sexauer's drug and confectionery store, and horseshoers M. A. Conrad, Henry Hoth and Albert Gautschy. In 1904, Frank Cook established a grocery, drygoods and meat market at the present 1144-6-8 Central Avenue, sold in 1908 to Charles Farren and Josiah Ward, who started a delivery service by horse and wagon. After another brief proprietorship, the store became the Wilmette Grocery in 1913, when owners Henry Fields and Louis Abraham took orders by the increasingly popular telephone.

As the business district expanded, Orner recalled, in about 1903, the Village board entered into a contract with the Welsbach Street Lighting Company for gas street lighting service, "which was improved upon from time to time by the addition of more modern burners . . ."

America's bicycle craze infected Wilmette, and the more daring riders made the challenging ride up, down, and around the sharp curves of the Hubbard Woods hill. Cyclists carried picnic baskets for a luncheon stop at Gage's pier.

After the Ouilmette Country Club's wooden building burned twice, members bought the land at the corner of Lake Avenue and Michigan and built a larger structure (now Michigan Shores Club), adding a golf course. Firemen held their annual picnic at Goldback's Grove on Lake Avenue west of Ridge Road. In 1908, as village clerk, Orner (who served as village president from 1925-1931) issued Wilmette's first automobile license to H. H. Hitchcock. His vehicle, manufactured in Kenosha, sped down the streets at 15 miles an hour.

The appearance of the new horseless carriages created an early suburban problem. Wilmette police stationed themselves along the busier streets on Sunday afternoon, fire hoses at the ready. Whenever an

112

automobile chugged past at a speed that seemed to exceed 12 miles an hour, the law-enforcement cadre would douse the hapless driver with a high-pressure stream of water.

One 1905 street sign warned, somewhat ungrammatically,

Automobile
Speed Limit 12 Miles Hour
Penalty for Violation of Ordinance
$25.00 to $200.00
All Vehicles Must Display Lights Night

But it was to be another decade before the upstart automobile would relegate Old Dobbin to oblivion.

In 1901, Horace G. Drury and J. M. Johnson urged the community to establish a lakefront park district, but the concept was not to become a reality for seven years. Patent attorney Louis K. Gillson was named the first president of the park district in 1908, to serve with great dedication until his retirement in 1934. In July, 1909, the district built a bath house, (financed by the contributions of residents) at the foot of Chestnut Street, and hired a full-time beach master. A year earlier, the idea of a park organization had been presented by Col. Robert R. McCormick, then president of the Chicago Metropolitan Sanitary District (later to become editor and publisher of the *Chicago Tribune*). The District was established by Illinois in 1889, and in 1905, as part of a drainage canal system, work began on the North Shore Channel and its Wilmette terminal. In 1909, the Wilmette harbor was built at the mouth of the channel by a young engineer named Edward J. Kelly, later mayor of Chicago.

Wilmette's First Closed Automobile, Date Unknown. The Peerless with side curtains and hand crank was owned by H. H. Hitchcock. Road is still unpaved.

Wilmette Promotional Advertisement, 1910. A page in Hill's Reference Guide to Evanston and Other Illinois Towns on the North Shore refers to Wilmette's natural beauty and residential advantages. The McGuire & Orr advertisement price range of homes is interesting as a comparison of real estate 66 years ago.

First New Trier High School Student Body, 1901. Faculty and students pose in front of newly-completed building after high school opened for classes in February, 1901.

Frank Smith's Grocery, Circa 1904. The Wilmette Directory for 1898 locates the store "on W. Railroad av 3rd n of Wilmette av" and the awning says 607. Building at right housed post office. Today, 607 houses the Wilmette Bicycle & Sport Shop.

Henry Hoth's Blacksmith
and Horseshoeing Shop,
Circa 1910. Now a cleaning
shop at 1827 Wilmette Avenue,
the establishment included
blacksmith Henry Hoth,
foreground, and his two
sons in aprons, Charles,
third from left, and
William. Boy with switch
to shoo away flies and men
at left are unidentified.
Photograph loaned by Mrs.
William (Catherine Hoth)
Henrich, granddaughter, who
recalls visiting the shop in
1919 with her Logan School
kindergarten class, each
child receiving a new
horseshoe nail as a souvenir
of the visit.

The New Trier Commercial
Association, Circa 1900.
Predecessor of Wilmette
Chamber of Commerce, this
picture was taken at the
annual picnic.

1916 Advertisement.

Van Deusen's Grocery and Market, Circa 1914.
Posing behind a tempting array of fresh fruit are employees of the store, 1154 Central Avenue, now occupied by the LP3 Shoppe. (Courtesy Henry Hoffman, second from left, front row).

1908 Advertisement.

Wilmette Meat Market, Circa 1905. The store, here probably pictured with July 4th decorations, was located on Ridge Road, just south of Lake Avenue. Lady customer and butchers are not identified.

Klinge & White Market, Gross Point, Circa 1914. Located just south of Ridge Road and Lake Avenue, in the heart of the Gross Point business district, owners and employees pose for this picture, taken the same day as the photo above: J. Schaefgen, Jeb Rau, George White, Harry Hiest, W. M. Klinge. Boy near center is Ralph Klinge; child at right is unidentified.

Southwest Corner, Lake &
Ridge Road, Gross Point,
Circa 1914.

1911 Advertisement.

Thanks-
giving
Turkeys

We have arranged to secure a large supply of fine Turkeys for
Thanksgiving which we will furnish our customers live or dressed.
Place your orders early.

KLINGE & WHITE

Telephone - - Wilmette 430

View Looking South on
Ridge Road, Gross Point,
Circa 1912. Busscher's
General Store seems popular
with the youngsters.

Wilmette Avenue and Central, Circa 1905. The fountain built by the Wilmette Woman's Club for both man and horse is in left foreground. McGuire and Orr Block is on the left, and the Brown Building has not yet been built. Streets are as yet unpaved.

Livery Service Advertisement, 1898. Located in what is now an entirely residential neighborhood at 16th Street and Columbus Avenue (now Walnut Avenue), early taxi service also rented "gentle horses for ladies."

Paul's. *Established 1894*

Livery and Boarding Stable

Columbus Av. and 16th St.
WILMETTE, ILL. Five Minutes' Walk Southwest of the Kenilworth Depot.......

Telephone ...Wilmette 31

Carriages Delivered and called for at any residence in Wilmette, Llewellyn Park, Kenilworth and Grosse Point.. .....*Gentle Horses for Ladies* a Specialty

BAGGAGE HANDLED PROMPTLY
To and From Trains....'Phone Me

Prompt Attention to Mail, Telephone or Telegraph Orders

Trains Made Day or Night on Order

Frank M. Paul
PROPRIETOR

3-Seated Surreys
8-Pass. Wagonettes
12-Pass. Wagonettes
....For Excursions
and Picnics

Col. McCormick told the Men's Club of Wilmette that the soil then being excavated in the digging of the North Shore Channel would be dumped into the lake between the inlet and Washington Avenue. By law, man-made land unoccupied and within the boundaries of an organized park district could be taken for park purposes. Wilmette, he said, would be wise to move promptly and acquire the 22 acres to be created.

In February, 1910, Northwestern University gave the park district the north 100 feet of the block and the 70 feet north of Forest Avenue to add to the 200 feet already owned near Lake Avenue, and Ouilmette Park became a reality. In December, 1911, the park board bought for $5,000 the land on the west side between Lake Avenue and Park and Fifteenth Street, naming this second park Vattman, for Father, later Monsignor, Edward J. Vattman, World War I army chaplain and close friend of President Theodore Roosevelt. Six years later another bathing beach was opened to village residents, at first manned by volunteers, then turned over to the park district for better management.

Wilmette's financial base was strengthed in 1905, when five men founded the Wilmette Exchange Bank, operating in the home of Clinton C. Collins at 1501 Forest Avenue. The first public facility followed at 1222 Central Avenue, and a year later the bank moved to 1200 Central, becoming in 1920 the Wilmette State Bank, with a new building.

Residents in 1900 were reading the *North Shore Record*, a four-page paper selling for three cents, "devoted to the interests of the North Shore in General and Wilmette, Kenilworth and the Township of New Trier in Particular." The news stories in one of the few surviving issues, dated September 15, 1900, capture the

View of the Park on the Lake Front, Circa 1905. The gentleman looking out towards the lake seems oblivious to the three ladies in white high button shoes and summer dress posing self-consciously on the park bench.

In the Park Lake Front

Drainage Canal Bridge, About 1908-1910. View is from the west, and shows a utility boat and bridge lights as they are today.

spirit of the day. Sheridan Road Day was to be celebrated October 8 when the route was opened, with a drive (preumably of buggies not autos) from Chicago to Lake Forest, with luncheon and events planned at the North Shore villages along the way. One article related the reluctance of Wilmette citizens to pay for cement paving, beginning to replace the old boardwalks, believing that their neighbors across the street should pay because they had used the boardwalks when it was the practice to build a walk on only one side of a street. A letter to the editor offered the solution: Wilmette, like Winnetka, should build the new paved walks on *both* sides of the street.

Will Gage's Pier and Beach Area, 1905. The wooden structure on the right, a fishing shack, washed away two years later.

In 1907, the Chicago, Milwaukee & St. Paul Railway leased its tracks to the Northwestern Elevated Railway of Chicago, which assumed operations up to Wilmette's Llewellyn Park. In 1910, the Northwestern Elevated acquired the right to the line, and started the present Rapid Transit Service, linking Linden Avenue with Chicago. That year, Wilmette's trustees asked the Chicago & North Western Railway to elevate its tracks through Wilmette, at the same time that the tracks were being elevated through Evanston, but they were not successful.

A positive sign of the change from pioneer village to Chicago suburb was provided in 1910 by Rev. Joseph W. Fogarty, rector of St. Augustine's Church. Fogarty sent a letter to the Village board denouncing "the

Wilmette Beach, 1916. Striped umbrellas helped protect against the sun, and concession hut featured Coca-Cola. Attire also helped shield wearers from the sun's rays.

"The Village Movie,", August 12, 1916. An 8-page newsletter, published weekly, advertising the week's features at both the Village and Central Theaters, featured stories about the stars, some local news items, advertising, and, occasionally, "extras." The April 21, 1917, issue invited residents to "Come and see yourself and neighbors on the screen," an "extra" for Wednesday and Thursday being the pictures made the previous week at the official opening of Sheridan Road.

The Village Theatre Program

September 11 to 16

Admission—Adults 15c; Children 10c

1150 Wilmette Avenue   Telephone Wilmette 1441

MONDAY Evening 7.00 8.20 9.30	MARY MCLAREN IN "SHOES" Biggest heart interest story of the age	BLUEBIRD
→	Extra—"From Carlsbad to Moravia"—Burton Holmes	
TUESDAY Matinee 3.30 p.m. Evening 7.00 8.20 9.30	MARY PICKFORD IN "HULDA OF HOLLAND" Quaint humor, will appeal to all	Paramount
→	Extra—"Farmer Al Falfa's Egg-Citement"—Bray Cartoon	
WEDNESDAY Evening 7.00 8.20 9.30	CLIFFORD BRUCE and DOROTHY GREEN IN "THE DEVIL AT HIS ELBOW" A play of romance and thrills	METRO PICTURES CORP'N
→	Extra—"Preparedness"—Sidney Drew Comedy	
THURSDAY Evening 7.00 8.20 9.30	WALLACE REID and CLEO RIDGLEY IN "THE HOUSE OF THE GOLDEN WINDOWS" Love, excitement and happiness	Paramount
→	Extra—"Paramount Pictographs"—Magazine on the Screen	
FRIDAY Evening 7.00 8.20 9.30	WILLIAM S. HART IN "THE CAPTIVE GOD" Story of the conquests of Montezuma, ruler of the Aztecs	
→	Extra—"Laundry Liz"—Triangle-Keystone Comedy	
SATURDAY Matinee 3.30 p.m. Evening 7.00 8.20 9.30	DE WOLF HOPPER and BESSIE LOVE IN "STRANDED" Story of small town and stage life	
→	Extra—"The Surf Girl"—Triangle-Keystone Comedy	

coming of the moving pictures and vaudeville theater . . . into this community" and urged the board to "suppress the same" in the theater at 1150 Wilmette Avenue. Now the J. Clarke Baker building, the Village Theater survived the rector's concerned opposition. In the February 26, 1916, issue of *The Local News* it was rated "first in elegance, size and general high character," seating 600 with wide aisles, and providing "only feature pictures of the best producing companies." Music for the silent movies was provided on a large Kimball pipe organ, somewhat unusual for a small community where the silents were usually accompanied by piano. The Village and Central theaters (The Central Theater was then at 1120 Central Avenue), managed by M. L. Sparr, were air cooled in summer and fumigated once a week with "solidified formaldehyde." Movies to be shown were listed in a weekly pamphlet mailed to residents, and included short items about the stars of the time to build a regular clientele from Wilmette's 4,943 residents.

In or about 1912, Wilmette's lakefront bluff area near Elmwood Avenue was the site for a commercial movie, about which historical files have virtually no information. A few still photographs have survived, showing Indians and a pioneer with musket, but the time, actual year, and theme or story line are not known.

As the village grew residentially and commercially, so did the need for adequate fire protection. In April, 1906, Walter H. Zibble was hired as the only paid member of the volunteer force, to be the fire wagon driver. The village was trying out a ladder wagon and team of horses bought a few days earlier in Evanston. The wagon replaced the hand-drawn hose

Wilmette's On-location Silent Movie, Circa 1912. Little information is available about the title, historic period or plot, except for these still photographs, probably of professional actors. Some of the scenes were photographed on the Elmwood Avenue bluff.

Ouilmette Country Club, First Village Club. The club was located at Ninth Street and Ashland Avenue, with its approach through the woods on a wooden sidewalk.

carts, and the fire department was housed at 1233 Central Avenue, now the site of the post office. One of the early fires in 1908 burned the Hoffmann store at Wilmette Avenue and Ridge Road to the ground. In 1918, two years after the department bought a motorized fire truck, the Kutten Brothers garage at 733 Green Bay Road was destroyed, the $1 million loss including 25 automobiles.

In 1910, Wilmette built its second village hall, an imposing peristyle structure with Grecian columns, designed by architect Henry J. Schlacks and completed at a cost of $27,500 under Village President John D. Couffer. Hardware merchant A. C. Wolff purchased the old hall for $1,500 and moved the building to 625 Park Avenue, remodeling it for use as a private home. That year, Troop 1, Boy Scouts of America, was organized as the first scout troop west of the Allegheny mountains in the back yard of Alonzo J. Coburn, who became assistant scoutmaster in October, as chief aide to scoutmaster Arthur L. Rice. The troop met Saturdays in the Congregational Church basement, using the English scouting handbook until the first American edition was available. When the troop had 120 boys, a second troop was formed at the Methodist Church.

Almost at the beginning of the decade, Wilmette and the neighboring suburbs realized the dream of their own township high school. On February 4, 1901, New Trier High School opened its doors to 76 pupils and seven teachers. Named for Trier, Germany, from which many of the Gross Point village citizens came, the school began in one building with a tower, surrounded by a field, woods, and swamp. Early Winnetka Avenue was a muddy road. The teachers and students ate in the basement beneath the front stairs, until enterprising

J. A. Hoth's Ice Wagons, Circa 1908. Wilmette children welcomed the wagons' approach on hot summer days with "Here comes the wagon!" Pictured here, from left, are John Feigen, Ed Ludlow and Henry Feigen (center wagon), and Jacob A. Hoth (standing), company owner, and Charley Mensel. Photograph was taken near barn behind Hoth home at 1204 Lake Avenue. Ice was delivered in 25, 50, 75 and 100-pound cakes, according to card placed in front windows of customers' homes.

Wilmette Fire Department and Ladder Wagon, Circa 1907. Wagon was purchased in 1905 from the Chicago Apparatus Company. Before 1906, when a pair of horses was bought for the department, horses were borrowed for $5. Driver is Walter H. Zibble, later Wilmette fire marshal, who was the only paid fireman among the volunteers.

students cooked hot dishes in the janitor's office.

Until 1912, books were kept in the rear of the third floor assembly hall, then a 1,200 book library was established. An east wing, used for manual education, was built in 1906. Later, an auditorium, dining hall, natatorium, and gymnasium were added. Frank L. Smart was the first superintendent (1900-1902), followed by Edward Manley (1902-1904), Bertrand D. Parker (1904-1905), Walter S. Asher and Elizabeth E. Packer (1905-1906), Frederick L. Sims (1906-1910), and Henry E. Brown (1910-1918).

In May, 1912, the *Lake Shore News* was started to cover the entire North Shore area. Four years later, after several publications were consolidated, the *News* covered only Wilmette and Kenilworth. In 1922, the name *Wilmette Life* was chosen in a contest, and the village had its own weekly publication.

In March of 1913, the Woman's Catholic Club was founded at the Ouilmette Country Club, and at the first meeting in April at St. Francis Xavier School at Ninth Street and Linden Avenue, Mrs. Peter J. Cuneen was elected president. Club members made thousands of dressings during World War I, working in the Central Theater building, now the Wilmette Theater.

Although by 1916 the park district had acquired the filled land for a lakeside park, the beach area was a clutter of fishermen's shacks, rotting pilings, and short piers. Wilmette Woman's Club president Mrs. Donald Gallie had admired Highland Park's attractive beach and studied its operation, and asked a neighbor, Mrs. George Martin, to head a beach committee and start an association which would collect fees, buy beach equipment, and hire guards. The one hitch seemed to be one of pre-World War I modesty; concern about people

WILMETTE FIRE DEPT. 1916.

Wilmette Fire Department, 1915, 1916. Top photograph shows the crew with a horse-drawn ladder wagon in 1915. Photograph below, taken one year later, shows firemen with the new chain drive fire truck, then the latest in fire fighting mechanization. Both photographs were taken in front of the Wilmette Theater, now the J. Clarke Baker Building.

Ouilmette Country Club
Minstrel Show program for
April 18 and 19, probably
1911. A five passenger Paige
36 touring car was advertised
for $1275.

Ouilmette Country Club,
Second Building, Circa 1909.
The second clubhouse was a
larger, more impressive
structure than the first
building, but was built on the
east side, at Lake and
Michigan Avenues.

His Workroom

Thomas Slater Gillette, Wilmette's Pioneer Photographer. Pictured in the basement workshop of his home at 830 Lake Avenue (the house has been replaced with the present two homes on the site), Gillette spent his working life in railroading and telegraphy, recalling at 87 he had been born in a log cabin from which wolves and deer could be shot from the doorway. Gillette, who died in August, 1939, at 92, took many of the Wilmette street scenes from 1902-1910.

Ye Olde Towne Folkes Annual Meeting, 1917. Posing in various period costumes at the meeting, held in the Brown Building hall in April, 1917, are, from left, John Page, Mrs. S. A. Wheelock, Myra Barker, Mrs. John Gage, Mrs. Susie Gage, Mrs. Byron C. Stolp, Mrs. F. L. Joy, Bertha Wheelock, and Mrs. Grace Wheelock Burge.

Brown Building, From Wilmette Avenue, 1916. During World War I, military personnel from Great Lakes and Fort Sheridan were housed overnight on the third floor, and dances were held in the ballroom on that floor.

1908 Advertisement.

SHIPLEY'S ORCHESTRA WILMETTE

THE BEST MUSIC FOR THE LEAST MONEY
WITH DRUMS AND BELLS
WE ARE "THE" IDEAL DANCE
ORCHESTRA. TRY US.
Telephone 2354
1444 Wilmette Avenue, - Wilmette, Illinois

in beach attire walking in the park on the bank above. It was finally agreed that bathers could walk in the park if covered by a robe or coat, and the park district soon took over the operation of the beach, developing regulations and policies and setting summer fees for Wilmette users.

World War I saw Wilmette boys march off to the conflict in Europe, and the organization of the Home Guard, commanded by New Trier Township collector Hoyt King. North Shore Company D of the Illinois Reserve Militia was organized, commanded by Capt. Arthur E. Howard, and Wilmette men made up a large portion of Company K. Mrs. Elizabeth Brooks, then Elizabeth Brown, recalls that in 1917, dances for soldiers and sailors from Fort Sheridan and Great Lakes were held in the third floor hall in her father Melville Brown's building, given by the War Camp Community Service.

"Often a boy or two with weekend leave would be offered a cot there and my father would bring them breakfast coffee and sweet rolls from Mrs. Wilson's bakery across the street," Mrs. Brooks remembers.

Wilmette residents did their share for the war effort, buying Liberty bonds and war savings stamps in

Wilmette Officers, Illinois Reserve Militia, 1919. Discharged village members of Company D pose sometime in 1919 for a photograph. Commander of the unit was Capt. Arthur H. Howard, second row, center. Pictured are: First row, from left - Corp. D. R. Brower, Corp. S. W. Lusted, Corp. J. V. Siever, Company Clerk E. P. Fatch, Sgt. J. A. Topp, Corp. M. P. Vore, Jr.; middle row - Capt. R. H. Rice, First Lt. J. R. MacFarland, Capt. A. H. Howard, Lt. G. L. Wire, Lt. H. J. Leach; Top row - Corp. M. H. McMillen, Corp. Harry Hamill, First Sgt. E. S. Hanson, Sgt. I. C. Nitz, Sgt. G. W. Carrington, Corp. C. K. Sanders, Quartermaster Sgt. L. A. Bower, Corp. H. A. Brown, Sgt. K. D. King, Corp. S. C. Bennett.

Wilmette Home Guard, 1918. In these photographs, Home Guard members line up in front of the Village Hall facing Wilmette Avenue and present arms in salute to the flag.

schools. In April, 1918, the *Lake Shore News* reported the establishment of a cadet training camp for New Trier boys at Lake Geneva, to teach them "trench warfare, trench digging, bayonet practice, scouting, skirmish fighting, and all the picturesque and exciting methods of modern warfare." Boys slept in tents, wore uniforms, and could go for one of several two-week periods from mid-June to mid-August. That May, Village President Edward Zipf, attorney Ralph Potter, and board members agreed to work without pay, to add $3,000 to the Village funds for other expenses, Zipf said, "as an example of interest in the welfare of the Village." One note of accusation came that month from Phil A. Grau, secretary of the Wilmette Guard, who called those who threw away food substitutes, bought to get white flour, "in a class beneath the pro-German propagandist and German secret service operative."

The war years saw the election of Wilmette's first woman trustee, Mrs. Estella M. Pierson, who served until 1919. A pioneer schoolteacher and Iowa native, she had been a charter member of the Woman's Club and several times president as well as president of the First Methodist Church and school board member.

The first two decades of Wilmette's twentieth century closed with a bit of excitement. On a July morning in 1919, a lone gunman entered the Wilmette State Bank, just opened for business, and pushed a note reading "Pay to the bearer all you have" across the window to assistant cashier William D. Leary. Leary stalled for time, and the would-be robber fired a shot, but missed. When Leary ducked and the bank employees fled to the back room, the bandit ran out of the bank. Leary called policeman Sam Hoth, who gave chase in a commandeered taxi, there being no squad car at that time. Hoth caught the man, later identified as Peter Swanson, and in an exchange of shots wounded the bandit three times. Swanson then shot himself in the head, and died a few hours later at Evanston Hospital.

The incident might have been a forewarning of the wave of lawlessness which was to characterize the 1920's and early 1930's, particularly in big cities like Chicago. Such incidents were to be almost non-existent in Wilmette, which by 1920 had again changed and become a comfortable, prosperous suburb, with all the facilities to make life pleasant for its residents.

Private Bernard Reinwald and Parents, 1918. Photograph taken in 1918 shows the Gross Point soldier with his parents, Joseph and Mary, pioneer Gross Point residents, shortly after he returned from combat service in France. Reinwald fought in the Somme, St. Michele and Meuse-Argonne offensives, was wounded, and received the Purple Heart for his courageous service. Now 83, he lives with his wife, Mary, in Northfield.

8

From Tornado to Depression: The 1920's

THE LAKE SHORE NEWS

Nearly Everybody In Wilmette Reads The Lake Shore News

VOL. VII, NO. 21. WILMETTE, ILLINOIS, FRIDAY, APRIL 2, 1920 SIXTEEN PAGES PRICE FIVE CENTS

Magnificent Trees and Beautiful Hall in Tornado Path

Sweeping Northwest in Wilmette Avenue, the Devastating Storm Laid Waste the Village Green and Carried a Portion of the Village Hall Roof for a Distance of Five Blocks, Shattering it to Splinters

Photo by William L. Lehle

WILMETTE RECOVER[illegible] FROM TORNADO S[illegible]K

Reconstruction Work in Full Progress; Business Houses Re-opened; Homes are Temporarily Repaired

TELEGRAMS FLOOD CITY

Scores of Messages Received from Anxious Relatives in All Parts of Country; Workers Praised

Like a war-ridden village of Belgium after the crushing heel of the invader had been lifted, tornado-swept Wilmette is preparing to resume its normal place in township activities.

A great part of the debris in the path of the tornado has already been cleared away and active steps taken for the alleviation of suffering of persons made homeless by the "death wind" which swept bullet-like through the heart of the village, smashing homes, snapping great trees like sticks and partially detroying public buildings and business places in the center of the Village.

Workmen Are Busy

Since Sunday afternoon every available carpenter, laborer and tradesman has worked day and night in the reconstruction work, with the result that most of the business houses are once more resuming their trade and citizens are again moving into their wrecked homes. The throngs of curiosity-seekers have disappeared almost entirely and the troops of Companies K and I of the Illinois National guard, who did excellent work in the storm-swept area, have been replaced by volunteer police while most of the citizens are going about their business as they did preceding the tornado.

Although no definite estimate of the damage will be available for some time, those who have made a thorough canvass of the devastated area believe the damage to residential and business districts will not exceed $200,000.

The Village hall, which was directly in the path of the tornado, suffered a heavy loss when the entire roof was ripped from the building and hurled four blocks to Ashland avenue and 7th street. The damage is estimated at about $15,000.

Churches Hard Hit

The roof of the Central hotel building has been temporarily repaired as has that of the Village hall. Among the churches the Episcopal and Lutheran edifices suffered most seriously, the former losing the entire upper part of the structure as the roof was smashed into chips.

Both the militia, the police and workers who aided in maintaining quiet and order after the tornado had swept through, and who took charge of the reconstruction work, came in for considerable praise from Edward Zipf, Village president. The prompt and efficient work of the corps of workers assigned to the various tasks of clearing away the wreckage and temporarily repairing business districts and homesteads was also highly commended.

Praise For Contractor

Central avenue business men joined this week in praising the heroic work of James Crabb, carpenter contractor, who appeared in the business section within an hour following the disaster prepared to board up window spaces and make temporary repairs requisite to saving the valuable stocks in the store buildings. Crabb furnished lumber, marshalled together his own workmen and asked only that the lumber be returned to his yards after permanent repairs had been completed. Crabb asked no remuneration for his services.

One of the heroes of the disaster was Earl E. Orner, station master and village clerk, who probably saved the lives of scores of passengers on a north-bound flyer by running down the tracks in the teeth of the gale to flag the train before it crashed into the fallen trees and wreckage on the tracks. Orner and station assitants worked in the storm clearing wreckage off the right of way.

Chief of Police E. G. Sieber and his men were also praised for their promptness in saving George Mix, gateman, from being burned alive in the wreckage of his shanty, after the tornado had whirled the shanty and gateman 50 feet across the tracks, pinning Mix under ruins of the cabin.

Residents of the village have been flooded all week with telegrams and telephone calls from all parts of the country from anxious friends and relatives.

Wilmette Population Computed at 7,824

Early Census Figures Published by Chicago Daily Place New Trier Township Population at 19,291

Early census figures announced this week by the Chicago Herald and Examiner show the population of New Trier Township (including villages and township territory proper) at 19,291, an increase of 8,414 over the figures of the census of 1910. Wilmette is now a thriving village of 7,825 residents, according to the published census, an increase in population of 2,881 or 58 per cent over the figures of 1910 which gave the village a population of 4,943.

Other census figures in New Trier Township give Glencoe 3,295 an increase of 74 per cent; Winnetka 5,115, an increase of 61 per cent and Kenilworth 992, an increase of 13 per cent. The population of New Trier outside the villages is given as 2,065.

RUMMAGE SALE

The Ladies of the Neighborhood Circle of the Congregational church will hold a rummage sale next Thursday from 8 a. m. to 6 p. m. in the Brown building, on Wilmette avenue.

EDITOR WEBER RETURNS TO DESK; CALL HIM UP

Editor E. W. "Mike" Weber of The Lake Shore News is back on the job. He returned this week to assume active charge of the editorial department of the paper after an absence of eight weeks.

Mr. Weber recently recovered from a severe attack of pneumonia. He has suffered no ill after effects. His ears will be glad to listen to your new contributions and all suggestions concerning the most approved method of conducting his department. His eyes are bright and prepared to observe everything that's of general interest. His type key fingers (one on each hand) are in first class running order and prepared to grind out real peppy news stories.

Just call Mr. Weber. Phone Wilmette 1920 when you hear or observe something everyone should know.

CITIZENS OF WILMETTE!

Fifteen families in our Village are in desperate straits today. They are looking upon the ruins of homes which meant their all. They are brave, hard-working neighbors who suffered the brunt of the death wind's merciless attack. They need help NOW— Not tomorrow or next week, but NOW.

You are asked to contribute to a Loan. You are asked to do your part in providing a Relief Fund of $15,000 for Wilmette Tornado sufferers.

Listen to this remarkable achievement!

Twenty-seven men of Wilmette on Tuesday evening subscribed $3,600 in ten minutes! That means the rest of us must get together $11,400. We can do it now!

The Survey committee of the Wilmette Tornado Relief Fund has completed a thorough canvass of the devastated residential area. They found fifteen families in need of immediate financial assistance for the rehabilitation of their homes.

None of these people want charity. You are contributing to a Loan Fund to be applied to the reconstruction work on these homes. This fund will then be held in reserve as an Emergency Fund to meet possible catastrophies which may, in the future, come upon Wilmette.

Mail that check today. Make it payable to Fred A. Smith, treasurer, of the Wilmette Tornado Relief Fund and mail to the Finance committee, Wilmette Tornado Relief Fund, Village Hall, Wilmette.

DO IT NOW!

Finance Committee, Wilmette Tornado Relief Fund,

C. D. Worthington, chairman
Edward Zipf
Frank J. Seng
C. H. Smith
Louis K. Gillson.

Clear Out The Attic—Page 7

Going To Move? Read Page 7

Pastor-War Hero, at Local Sunday Club

Dr. Samuel N. Watson, Rector Emeritus of American Episcopal Church, Paris, France, Here April 4

Dr. Samuel N. Watson, Rector Emeritus of the American Episcopal church of Paris, France, will be the speaker before the Wilmette Sunday Evening club, April 4. The address will be appropriate to Easter.

The church which Dr. Watson represents is the largest of the denomination in all Europe, which in a measure indicates the importance of the man. He was active rector of the church until he came to America a few months ago. For two years prior to the beginning of the great war, he was in Paris, and he rendered most important service throughout the entire struggle.

Honored In War

Dr. Watson is Knight of the Legion of Honor of France, and of the Legion of Honor of Belgium, and was Commander of the Order of St. Saba of Serbia. He was vice president of the American Executive Committee for Fatherless Children of France of which General Joffree was president. He was also vice president of the American Ambulance Hospital in France.

The soloist of the evening will be Mrs. Alice W. Keilar, contralto.

On Sunday, April 11, the speaker before the Sunday Evening club will be the Rev. George Craig Stewart of Evanston. On April 18, the program will be in charge of Dean Peter Lutkin of the Music department of Northwestern University, who will direct the A Cappella Choir in a musical program.

EXPECT RECORD CROWD AT JUNIOR BASEBALL DANCE

The first informal dance given by the Wilmette Junior Baseball team will be held at the Wilmette Woman's club, Tenth street and Greenleaf avenue, Tuesday evening, April 6, at 8 o'clock. Good music is promised. Refreshments will be served.

The Junior boys expect to receive their baseball uniforms this week and practice on the new diamond at Third street and Linden avenue, is expected to begin within a few days.

Paul Schroeder, Real estate dealer, is credited with securing the east site playing field for the lads. The first game of the season is scheduled for April 18.

WILMETTE ASKED FOR $15,000 RELIEF FUND

Village Tornado Relief Fund Committee Prepared to Launch Work of Actual Reconstruction of Homes

27 MEN SUBSCRIBE $3,600

Devise Procedure in Loaning Funds To Families Destituted by Sunday Storm

Prompt action by Village President Edward Zipf in appointment of representative men of Wilmette as committee members of the Wilmette Tornado Relief Fund resulted in establishment of a definitely outlined procedure in the Relief work among Wilmette tornado sufferers.

Three committees have been busy every evening this week working and planning so effectively that, at a joint session at the Village Hall on Wednesday evening, all was placed in readiness for the actual home reconstruction work.

Report Conditions

The joint committee heard a report by chairman George R. Harbaugh of the Survey committee announcing that fifteen families of a total of forty-five were in need of immediate financial assistance. None of these families, he explained, would accept charity, but, rather, desired facilities for accepting loans. Mr. Harbaugh pointed out that $15,000 would be required to cover the combined amounts of such loans. Of that amount $3,600 was previously subscribed by twenty-seven men of the Village, most of them members of the joint committee.

Permanent Relief Fund

Following the report and a general discussion the committee decided, unanimously to loan the money on plain notes. The funds, it was further decided, would be placed in the Wilmette State Bank with Fred A. Smith, treasurer of the Relief fund, as trustee. All bills incurred in the reconstruction work, then, would be met by the Finance committee. Money returned by the borrowers, it was decided, should be retained as a permanent Relief and Emergency Fund for the Village.

The Village will not be canvassed for funds as at first proposed the joint committee deciding instead to make public a request for funds through the columns of The Lake Shore News. Attention of readers is directed to the center column of the First page, first section, of this issue of The Lake Shore News, for information regarding the correct procedure to be followed in subscribing to the Fund.

Fund Personell

Louis K. Gillson is general chairman of the Wilmette Tornado Relief Fund. Edward F. Kelley is secretary, and Fred A. Smith, treasurer.

Members of the committees are:

Executive Committee: Lyman M. Drake, chairman; Henry J. Haack, C. H. Smith, Charles S. McCoy.

Finance Committee: C. D. Worthington, chairman, Edward Zipf, Frank J. Seng, C. H. Smith, Louis K. Gillson.

Survey and Relief Committee: George R. Harbaugh, chairman, James Crabb, Charles Brethold, Earl E. Orner, Paul Schroeder, Harry Fowler, Dr. F. E. Moore.

WILMETTE MAN, REPAIRING STORM DAMAGE, KILLED

Another name was added to the heavy toll of deaths caused by Sunday's tornado Wednesday when John Taggart, 76 years old, a retired contractor, was killed in the back yard of his home, 1310 Isabella street, by a charged electdic wire. Mr. Taggart was repairing several small buildings in the rear of his home and accidently caught hold of a guy wire that was carrying a load of 2,400 volts. Mr. Taggart is survived by his wife, Mrs. Marie Taggart, and four children, John and Frank Taggart, Mrs. Bessie Cassidy, and Mrs. Lyda O. Harrison.

TRAIN HITS AUTO

One of the early morning commuter trains pulling out of the local depot yesterday morning struck the foreward part of an automobile which had been driven upon the tracks before the gates at the Wilmette avenue crossing could be lowered. The automobile was only slightly damaged and the driver disappeared before his name could be learned.

Tornado Issue of the Lake Shore News. Published the Friday following the Wilmette tornado of Palm Sunday, March 28, 1920, the News carried a front page photograph of damage to the Village Green, and an appeal to citizens to contribute $15,000 as a loan to homeless families.

Palm Sunday, March 28, 1920, began quietly enough. Wilmette families breakfasted, then left for church services in the chill, rainy morning, looking forward to spring and brighter days. Many were just returning home when the sky turned an ugly yellow and a torrential rain began. In the early afternoon, without warning, the deadly tornado struck, its violent, invisible hands sweeping like a juggernaut along Wilmette Avenue. It ripped the roof from Village Hall, carried it four blocks, and dropped it at Ashland Avenue and Seventh Street. St. Augustine's Episcopal Church lost its entire upper structure, smashed by flying debris which filled the air.

Huge trees were uprooted, plucked like weeds by the giant tornado's fist. Windows were blown in, telephone wires were festooned with curtains and household goods. Police rushed to rescue gateman George Mix from his blazing shanty, which had been hurled 50 feet across the railroad tracks and set afire by the upset stove. The tornado slammed into the Henry Gage house on Sheridan Road near Chestnut Street, but the venerable old house, then a restaurant, survived the blow, only to be demolished later, a victim of high taxes.

The Central Hotel was badly damaged, as were the stores along the west side of West Railroad Avenue. The tornado severely damaged the Lutheran Church, and in its few minutes of violence, 15 houses were destroyed and 45 more badly damaged. The ground was littered with debris and dotted with the remains of garages and small sheds the tornado had lifted and carried for blocks, then smashed to kindling. The April 20 tornado issue of the *Lake Shore News* likened the destruction to "a war-ridden village of Belgium after the crushing heel of the invader had been lifted."

Companies I and K of the Illinois National Guard were called in to maintain order, help clear the wreckage, and prevent looting. Wilmette officials quickly set up tents to feed the homeless, and citizens were asked to contribute $15,000 immediately as a loan to the 15 homeless families. To start the ball rolling, a group of 27 men pledged $3,600 in ten minutes at an evening meeting. Village president Edward Zipf appointed park district president Louis K. Gillson chairman of the Tornado Relief Fund, C. D. Worthington to head the Finance Committee, and George R. Harbaugh chairman of the Survey and Relief Committee. The *News* paid special tribute in its tornado issue to carpenter-contractor James Crabb, "who appeared in the business section within an hour following the disaster, prepared to board up window spaces and make temporary repairs," to protect merchants' valuable stock. Crabb used his own lumber and workmen, and asked no pay for his efforts.

Among the individual acts of heroism that Sunday was that of station agent Earl E. Orner, who raced down the railroad tracks "in the teeth of the gale" to flag down a passenger train before it could plow into the trees and other wreckage strewn along the tracks. The disaster left the village shaken, but determined to repair and rebuild as quickly as possible, and work began almost as soon as the tornado had blown itself out. But

Tornado of Palm Sunday, 1920. Views of the damage to the business district and private homes. First photograph looking northwest from the corner of Wilmette Avenue and West Railroad Avenue (Green Bay Road) shows Max Mueller's Market, now a restaurant, and Millen's Hardware store, now the Wilmette Bicycle Shop.

Second photograph looks through destroyed trees at the old Gage Mansion, then the Lake Shore Tavern, which was razed in the 40's. The restaurant was soon labeled "Tornado Tavern." Third photograph is of the John Schopen barn on Kline Street (now Prairie Avenue) south of Wilmette Avenue.

What the Tornado did at
Lake Shore Tavern
Mar. 28th, 1920.

Brook's
photo.

John Schopen's Barn
Tornado at Wilmette Ill.
Mar. 28th 1920

Palm Sunday, 1920, became an unforgettable part of Wilmette's history, and is remembered today by many of its citizens.

The decade of the 1920's was one of material and social progress. In 1921, a group of North Shore sailing buffs organized the Buccaneers' Club, to encourage sailing in small boats, particularly the club's fleet of 15-foot catboats. Members leased the replica of the *Santa Maria* caravel which had been displayed at Jackson Park harbor during the Columbian Exposition of 1893. In the spring, the boat would be brought north from its South Chicago anchorage to Wilmette Harbor, a floating clubhouse called "The Port of Missing Men." The boat had a kitchen and restaurant, and in 1923 members paid a $100 initiation fee ($50 for boat owners and junior members) and annual dues of $40. At least once, the caravel was crushed by ice and sunk, but it was always raised and repaired for parties aboard by members and families, or the occasional stag party held in late September, before the club closed for the winter and the boat was moved to the south side of Chicago.

In 1922, Wilmette Theater (once Central) owner George Siegel closed the theater, leaving moviegoers with only the Village Theater until the imposing Teatro del Lago opened in 1927 in No Man's Land. That year, Wilmette officials passed an ordinance which prohibited showing movies on Sunday. The declining admissions soon forced the Village Theater to close, leaving only the Teatro, until the Village reopened in 1930. In 1928, Wilmette residents saw and heard their first talking movie, "The Desert Song" with the sound from a record not always synchronized with the film action.

One of the most significant accomplishments during the decade was the Wilmette Plan of 1922, which set

Wilmette's Buccaneers' Club "Port of Missing Men", April, 1923. Photograph is from the Chicago Evening Post for April 27, 1923. The Buccaneer's Club was organized in 1921 to promote small boat sailing in the North Shore area, and leased the replica of one of Columbus' caravels which had been displayed in Jackson Park lagoon during the Columbian Exposition. The floating clubhouse featured social events from cards to suppers for members and wives, who evidently had no intention of allowing sailor husbands to be missing very long.

SAILORS PREPARE

forth an imaginative projection of needs and growth. The Plan Commission had been appointed in 1919, headed by chairman Edward L. Scheidenhelm, and in 1922 published its findings and recommendations in a handsome printed book. "The period of haphazard building, of hurried settlement, has passed," the text began. Noting that expansion could only be west (two years before Gross Point was annexed), the Plan noted the growth of Wilmette's population from 1,500 in 1880 to 7,814 in 1920, and used Evanston, Brookline and Newton, Mass., and New Rochelle and Mount Vernon, N.Y., as models to predict that Wilmette would grow to 13,000 in 1930, 20,000 in 1940, 29,000 in 1950, and 40,000 in 1960.

The Plan, 1922. Illustration at left is architect Charles C. Henderson's drawing of the central business district as it would appear when improvements and alterations suggested in the Plan were instituted. The Mall, shown in the Civic Center plan below, is somewhat similar in concept to the plan developed in the late 1940's.

PLAN OF THE PROPOSED WILMETTE CIVIC CENTER.

Zoning Map, 1922 Plan. At this time, the Village western limits were at Ridge Road.

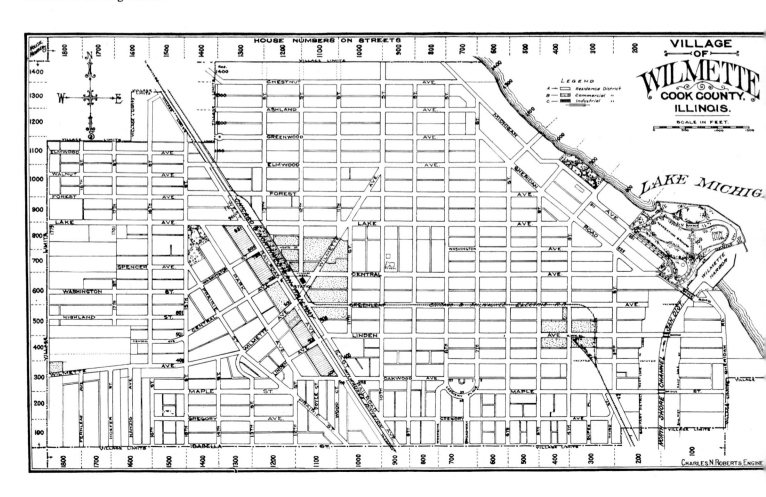

Illustrated with a color drawing were the proposed village green and memorial, elevated railroad tracks, mall and post office, and the need for additional sewers was voiced, if Gross Point should be annexed. The Village's gas lighting system with low candle power and 300 to 500-foot spacing were to be replaced with modern electric lighting, spaced 120 feet in the business section and 200 feet in residential areas, and with a refractor in each lamp to direct the light downward. Heavily traveled streets like West Railroad Avenue were to be reinforced with concrete, and truck loads would be limited and trucks themselves restricted to certain streets. The village green was to be off Wilmette Avenue opposite the Village Hall, and used not only as a public gathering place but also to present an attractive view to railroad passengers, as would the mall. Village plantings would be hawthorn, wild crab, and elm native to the area, and home builders were urged to respect the old trees. As the Plan said, "then our village will be a bower of blossoms and of graceful plantings."

Finally, the report suggested, a new junior high school was needed to relieve crowding, and warned that there be "no annexation of lands west of the present village limits" without a thorough study of roads, parks, sewerage, flood drainage, lighting and transportation, and water, to form a base for sound decisions and avoid "a haphazard growth which might prove detrimental to the best interests of the village."

All in all, the 1922 Plan was imaginative beyond its time, and with the notable exception of an elevated railroad (considered again in the late 1930's), and village green acquisition, many of the recommendations became accomplished points of progress within a relatively few years.

In 1922, a group of 40 Wilmette girls organized the first Girl Scout troop, with the help of Methodist pastor Dr. Gilbert Stansell. By the fall of 1929, the troop was meeting in a special room in the Methodist church, and members had returned from summer camping at Lake Geneva. In July of 1922, a small group of Wilmette gardeners met at the home of Mrs. B. L. Davis, 115 Third Street, to found the Wilmette Garden Club, whose first president was Mrs. David Cooke. Five years later, the club held its first garden market and plant sale, and took part in Chicago's first annual Flower Show.

Catholic girls could attend the high school opened in September, 1923 in the north wing of the Maria Immaculata Convent at 1041 Ridge Road. The school was named "The Mallinckrodt," and the convent complex, the mother house of the Sisters of Christian Charity, had been founded in 1916, when the Sisters came to Wilmette from the mother house at Wilkes-Barre, Pa. In 1918, the convent also housed a junior college, which was then a preparatory school for the Sisters' teaching careers.

One of Wilmette's most influential organizations was born in 1924, when Mrs. J. G. Wray, chairman of the civic and legislative committee of the Wilmette Woman's Club, organized the Wilmette League of Women Voters. The League was the local branch of the national League, and reflected the concerns of women who had won the right to vote just a few years earlier. Led by the first president, Mrs. Lloyd Ayres, the League started an active non-partisan program, working to promote political responsibility through informed and active participation of citizens in government.

In February, another Village organization, the

148

Save this Virgin Forest
To the Children *of* Wilmette

Civic Organizations in Move to Preserve Wilmette's Last Tract of Natural Forest

---

Why every citizen and property owner should support the effort to protect this beautiful woodland from destruction, that it may forever remain what it is today—nature's playground for the children, and a charming and distinguishing

Gateway to Wilmette

At the Gateway to Wilmette

What a village thinks of itself is shown by the appearance it presents to the eyes of the visiting outsider.

First impressions go a long way toward establishing a reputation with the

That is why any village, such as Wilmette which is primarily a village of homes if it has self-respect, if it wishes to build up a population of home-makers, neighborly, orderly, beauty-loving, with community pride and public-spirit, will

Save This Virgin Forest Pamphlet, Circa 1922. Undated article urges citizens to demonstrate support for park expansion and preservation by petitioning the Park Board to acquire the tract west of the tracks at Isabella and Green Bay, then called Main Street. A triangle bordered by Oakwood, Wood Court, Isabella and Main was threatened by rezoning for commercial use, and citizens' committee urged preserving it in its natural state. They were not successful.

Looking Southwest and Across Main Street

stranger. Evidences of appreciation for neatness and order and beauty attract those who love these things, and who, because of their love for them, are the most desirable type of residents.

take especial care of its gateways and approaches.

It will give to the visitor at first sight an impression that it cares proudly for its own appearance. It will not greet

THE DAYTON MOTORCYCLE

7 Horse Power $265
9 Horse Power $275

Power, Reliability, Cleanliness, Safety, Comfort, Economy, Flexibility

ROBERT McDANIEL
Wilmette Distributor
TELEPHONE 445

1916 Advertisement.

Wilmette News Agency, Circa 1923. Newspaper delivery was at least partly motorized by motorcycle in center, but delivery boys also relied then, as now, on pedal power.

Waukegan Express, Circa 1921. View is southeast from Fourth Street and Greenleaf Avenue, of northbound four-car train rounding the curve. (Courtesy George Campbell)

C.M.S. & M.R.R. Co., October, 1925. View is north from the Greenleaf Avenue curve. Village Hall has second story added after 1920 tornado. Site now the International House of Pancakes building and parking lot. (Courtesy Bill Robertson)

Advertisement for Wilmette-to-Chicago El.

Use the Elevated

TO

The Shopping District in Chicago

DIRECT TO THE DOORS OF CHICAGO'S GREATEST STORES

WITHOUT THE ANNOYANCE AND EXPENSE OF TRANSFER

DIRECT CONNECTIONS

From the **Loop Platforms** to

**SIEGEL COOPER & CO.
CARSON PIRIE SCOTT & CO.
ROTHSCHILD & CO.**

===== FARE 10 CENTS =====

Running Time 45 Minutes Wilmette to the Heart of Chicago's Shopping District

Northwestern Elevated R. R. Co.

Linden Avenue "L" Terminal, Circa 1925-30. Taxicabs lined up waiting for fares. Posters flanking door urge riders to "Relieve Street Congestion" by riding Chicago Rapid Transit. Station appearance is virtually unchanged today.

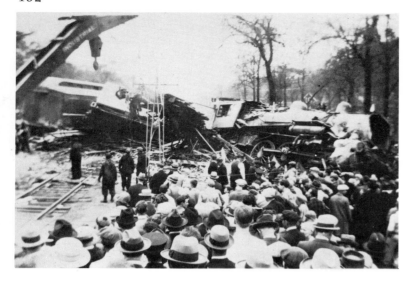

Chicago and North Western Railway Train Wreck, May, 1926. The rear-end collision between a southbound passenger train and a freight train about noon on May 21 caused four freight cars to derail and the locomotive of the passenger train to overturn. There were fortunately no injuries and the crew worked around the clock to clear the wreckage and open the tracks for service by the following morning. (Courtesy Harvey M. Hopp)

Wilmette Police Department, 1923. Posing with the department's three motorcycles, left to right, are Charles Lance, Henry Brautigan, William Kruel, Joe Steffens, Herman Vance, George Schaefer, Gottfried Ahrendt, Jack Schaefgen, Carl Greif, Peter Schaefer, Joe May, Lt. Albert Borre, and Chief Ed Sieber.

Wilmette Rotary Club, was founded, with banker Dan G. Stiles as president, printer and publisher Lloyd Hollister as vice president; realtor David E. Allen as treasurer; and banker William D. Leary as treasurer. One of the club's first projects was the organization and sponsorship of the Wilmette Community Chest in October, 1924, to combine the needs of civic and charitable groups under a single agency. The following March, an initial budget of $28,000 was approved, and under president Leslie F. Gates the first campaign was launched. Beneficiary organizations were the Arden Shore Association, Near East Relief, Red Cross, Salvation Army, and local charities not enumerated.

In the mid-1920's, Wilmette citizens could buy a snappy Essex Coach Super Six auto for $795 ($863 delivered) with a down payment of only $420, or a Hudson Coach for a heftier $1,288. A Ford Tudor Sedan in channel green with nickel-plated radiator was $580, the black touring model $290, and the Ford Runabout, also in black and including storm curtains, was a bargain at $260, though the starter was $85 extra. The new Brunswick Radiola with enclosed loudspeaker was $275 from the Wilmette Music Shop at 1179 Wilmette Avenue. And in that 1925 year, Wilmette and several of the other North Shore suburbs agreed to push plans for the expanded major north-south artery to be

called Green Bay Road, which would be a 40-foot-wide thoroughfare through the communities.

But a wider Green Bay Road and a booming market for automobiles were not without their problems. In a July 9, 1926, editorial, the *Wilmette Life* bemoaned the traffic congestion: "On pleasant holidays Sheridan Road and other important highways are all but jammed to a standstill." Almost as soon as business streets were widened, they were too narrow, the editorial observed, concluding that even though people had to park a block or two from shopping, "the auto is here to stay and increase in number."

On August 12, 1925, at 9 p.m., an event important to progress took place. The Village's new $305,000 electric lighting system glowed, as current was sent through the 1400 street lamps, marking the end of construction which had begun on March 27. For almost two years, contracts had been negotiated for power with the Sanitary District, a test block with models set up, a spacing of 130 feet determined, and lanterns with two reflectors bought from Westinghouse. The system included 180 large posts, 1171 small posts, 87 miles of underground cable, 30 large transformers, and 2400 feet of two-inch pipe to carry wiring under railroad crossings and pavement. The controlling station was (and is) the red brick building at Electric Place north of Central

Avenue, and west of the Wilmette Bank. Best of all, the project was completed six weeks ahead of schedule, by no means a common occurrence, then or now.

In August, 1926, Wilmette policemen were given a $10 monthly raise to $175, a salary equal to Evanston's scale. The Copeland electric refrigerator could be purchased for $215 in white with 108-cube capacity at John Millen's store at 1219 Wilmette Avenue. People were reading Anita Loos' *Gentlemen Prefer Blondes,* Carl Sandburg's *Abraham Lincoln,* and Mark Sullivan's *Our Times.* A Pierce-Arrow five-passenger two-door was $2,995, and in the June 18 issue of the *Wilmette Life,* realtor F. Coleman Burroughs at 1157 Wilmette Avenue advertised an "East Wilmette Bargain," an eight-room frame house with fireplace, heated porch, newly decorated, on a large lot "with fine old trees," two blocks from the North Western depot, all for $14,500.

There was evidently a concern that Wilmette was too costly a suburb for young couples. In an April, 1926, *Life* article, Village Board member C. E. Drayer said that young marrieds "can live in Wilmette in a small single home built for $4,000 cost and in the newly annexed territory, on a small lot as low as $1,500, so that the total costs would not be over $6,000." Drayer argued that it was no harder "for our young people today to build a house in Wilmette than for their parents 20 years ago," warning that there was no valid reason for "ever admitting flats into Wilmette" and that developers "need constant watching" because of their commitment to profit.

Several newsworthy events occurred in 1926. On April 20, citizens voted to annex 1,500 acres of Skokie Valley land west of the Village limits, by a two-to-one margin, an action supported earlier by the Chamber of

Commerce which warned that the alternative might be to see the area become an eyesore of shacks. In that same vote, Wilmette approved a Recreation Board to coordinate Village facilities under one central program, with John Clark Baker as chairman. The new Recreation Board hired Daniel Davis from Terre Haute as the first director, and began its duties by managing intra-village sports and the winter and summer playground programs.

Several days of excitement were provided by the Friday, May 21, Chicago and North Western train wreck, just north of Lake Avenue. At noon, the southbound passenger train rammed the rear of a freight train, demolishing four freight cars and the locomotive of the passenger train, and strewing debris along the right of way. After dispersing the inevitable crowd of onlookers (including New Trier students let out for the afternoon), a railroad crew cleared the wreckage by the following morning.

That September, members of Wilmette Lodge 931, A.F. and A.M., moved into their new Masonic Temple at 1010 Central Avenue, a permanent home 18 years after the first meeting to form a lodge in January, 1908.

The third event of that 1926 year was to cast a long shadow. A group of North Shore men and one woman proposed a plan to develop the area known as No Man's Land along Sheridan Road between the Kenilworth border and Chestnut Street. It was an area unpoliced, unrestricted, and under no municipal control. Wilmette residents immediately rose in opposition, and formed a committee under chairman Arthur Bonnet to call a referendum for the issuance of $500,000 in bonds to acquire the strip for park land. Urged to act "as patriotic citizens of the community" and drop the plan, the developers politely said they were patriotic but also knew what they were doing. Bonnet wrote to them again, concerned that the

Commercial Trucks of A. M.
Ryckoff, 1924. Photograph
does not identify location,
but railroad car is passing in
right background. Trucks and
tractor at left have hand
cranks, and contractor's truck
at left was used to transport
window glass.

Advertisement, The Local
News, 1920. Stucco was a
very popular modernization
at this time.

Once a Frame Shanty
—now a beautiful stucco residence

Look at this new and attractive bungalow!
You wouldn't believe that it was once an old
weather-worn wooden house — beyond the
hope of the owner!

It was covered with *Kragstone Stucco*. Now it is one of
the most beautiful homes in the community — distinctive,
fireproof and permanent.

If your building needs remodeling — if it is constructed of
wood, brick or concrete, let us tell you how we can make
it BETTER THAN NEW at very small cost!

KRAGSTONE STUCCO

You'll be surprised at the results. Choose any color or finish
you wish. The house will always look new and clean. Kragstone is a magnesite stucco — it will not crack or discolor.

Be sure to ask us to show you samples and give you an estimate on the cost of remodeling your house. *No time like
the present.*

Central Coal & Material Co.
2 02 West Railroad Avenue   EVANSTON
Phone: Evanston 5200   Phone: Wilmette 333

unaffiliated area would attract "thousands of people
nightly, on amusement bent," to see the Sunday night
movies at the planned Teatro del Lago Theater. A move
by the citizens committee to have an Illinois bill passed
to compel Wilmette to acquire the land was defeated,
and the developers began to let contracts to build two
clubs, the Vista del Lago and the Breakers Beach Club,
the Teatro del Lago theater, the Miralago ballroom,
apartments, and a motor arcade in the Spanish-style
shopping center.

Although some memberships in the Breakers were
sold, the structure was never finished because of the
Depression, and for years the cement staircase and lower
level stood on the beach. The Vista del Lago was
planned as a yacht club, but it, too, was never finished,
although it was used for a time for boat moorings. The
Miralago was finished, with shops on the ground floor
and an elegant ballroom above. Designed by architect
George Fred Keck, the ballroom had silvered ceilings,
green draperies, black marble columns, murals, and a
lighting system that changed colors. Music was by the
Dell Coon orchestra, and Richard Penney, head of the
Miralago Corporation, assured the North Shore that the
ballroom would be a completely wholesome place,
allowing no lone males or unescorted women, charging
admission for the evening rather than by the dance, and
prohibiting liquor or setups. Penney promised that his
ballroom would cater to "the young people of the
North Shore area who seek sound diversion under the
most wholesome auspices." The grand opening was July
12, 1929, but less than three years later the ballroom
and shops were destroyed by a March fire, to which fire
equipment was not sent in time because of the location
in unincorporated No Man's Land.

Wilmette Day Parade, 1927.
Returning to a decorated
horse-drawn carriage for the
parade in September are,
from left, Paul Bleser, Jr.,
Joseph Bleser, Miss Anna
Huerter, Mrs. Harry Leis, and
Robert Evans. Location of
photograph is unknown.

Wilmette League of Women Voters, Circa 1929. Officers pose for a sepia photograph in the *North Shore Graphic*. First names were not given in the caption, but League president Mrs. Shelby Singleton is seated, center

If the buildings in No Man's Land were ill-fated, the Teatro del Lago theater was the exception. On Saturday evening, April 23, 1927, the theater opened with "Afraid to Love," starring Florence Vidor and Clive Brook. Owner Samuel Meyers promised to show courtesy to patrons and to book choice films, including D. W. Griffith's "Sorrows of Satan," "Tell It to the Marines," "The Kid Brother," and the Greta Garbo-John Gilbert classic, "Flesh and the Devil." Perhaps the latter offering, an X-rated film of its day, created apprehension among the citizens. In a full-page advertisement in an April issue of the *Wilmette Life*, the

Panorama, Wilmette Harbor, Circa 1925. This view, published in a Wilmette Chamber of Commerce brochure about the village, shows the replica of the Santa Maria, used by the Buccaneers' Club, the studio-residence of Benjamin Marshall, and, interestingly, a seaplane in the middle of the harbor. At this time, the U.S. Coast Guard Station was still located at the Grosse Point Lighthouse in Evanston.

Benjamin Marshall Residence, Circa 1926. The flat-roofed, bauhaus-style mansion overlooking the Wilmette Harbor was designed by architect Benjamin Marshall for his studio-residence, and was lavishly designed of granite; containing five fireplaces and a black onyx bathtub with gold faucets, it also featured an outdoor swimming pool. Mr. Marshall, architect of

both the Edgewater Beach Hotel and Drake Hotel, was best known for his gold coast apartment buildings. Sold to the Goldblatt family in the 30's, it was offered to the village as a gift when taxes soared, but it was not accepted, and was razed. Only the iron gates remain, now part of the Baha'i properties.

New Trier Citizens' Committee warned of the Sunday movies in the strip, and urged voters to support passage of Illinois House Bill 51, which would authorize annexation of No Man's Land by Wilmette, creating needed control and providing tax revenues. But the movement was not to be successful for many years, and the Sunday movies continued to draw large audiences.

As the decade drew to a close, the Wilmette People's Party advertised its platform for the April 19, 1927, election, calling for opposition to flats; a franchise and payment for the use of streets used by the Chicago, North Shore and Milwaukee Railroad; elevation of the Chicago and North Western Railway tracks through Wilmette; a garbage disposal plant; and opposition to a village manager as costly and unsuitable. Voters evidently agreed, supporting the party's candidate, Earl Orner, against the Home Party by a vote of 3,092 to 1,558.

On the eve of the stock market crash late in 1929, the Wilmette Music Shop advertised the Majestic radio for $116 and $146, Van Deusen's grocery was selling 10 bars of American Family soap for 70 cents, 75 percent of New Trier High School's 1929 graduates had entered 81 colleges, and Charles Shantz Dingee, son of pickle pioneer Samuel Dingee, died on January 22, 1930, at 69.

9

Depression and War Years:
1930-1950

Aerial Views of East Wilmette area, May and July, 1930. Only the circular foundation of the Baha'i Temple has been completed (upper right) and the Gillson Park area is almost bare of trees. Linden Avenue elevated station is in the center at the Fourth Street and Linden Avenue intersection in top photograph. Bottom photograph is a closer view of harbor and park area.

Wilmette reacted quickly to the Stock Market Crash of October 29, 1929, and the severity of the Great Depression which followed Black Tuesday, binding the nation in a grip of fear and economic chaos. The early years of the 1930's were to be a mixture of economic concern for the jobless, the scarcity of funds to meet school budgets, and the needs of the community for organizational change and new institutions.

An early symptom of the Depression in Wilmette was the question of how to meet the school budgets. The *Wilmette Life* for February 28, 1930, headlined the story that funds to pay Village teachers and maintain the schools, as well as the New Trier faculty, were about exhausted. Worse, attempts had failed to secure a loan of the $650,000 needed in tax warrants from both local and Chicago banks. Chicago banks were not inclined to continue loans to outlying areas, and Wilmette's financial institutions had already bought their limit of the warrants. A campaign was started to get the support of residents, who were asked to buy tax warrants in denominations of $100 and up from the banks. Wilmette resident William H. Ellis was appointed campaign chairman, and the March 27 issue of the *Life* reported that schools would not shut down.

Even before the campaign could be launched, residents bought enough warrants to make a public drive unnecessary, although the initial subscription left the schools in a cliffhanger situation with enough money to operate only through March. Money continued to be received, and the crisis was averted, only to recur two years later. That March, Village President Earl L. Orner was asked to submit a plan to the board for creation of a village manager position. Those who favored the

village manager system pointed to the growth of the community and the need for a paid professional head with technical and practical experience, as in Winnetka, Glencoe and Kenilworth. But it was several years before the first paid village manager was appointed to administer Wilmette affairs.

In April, 1930, Wilmette began to accept bids on a huge storm sewer system for the area west of Ridge Avenue, with a projected cost of $1,804,950 and an April 15 deadline for bids. The new system was to include 26 miles of sewers, and a pumping station north of Lake Avenue near the north boundary of the Chicago River, because it was against Chicago Metropolitan Sanitary District regulations to dump water into Lake Michigan.

Wilmette saw the birth of two new organizations in that unlikely year. The Northridge Woman's Club was founded in the rapidly growing residential area of northwest Wilmette, with Mrs. P. Jay Church as president, to study community problems and to improve the Village. By 1933, the Club included a literary group, was conducting parliamentary law classes, and had a garden committee, and in 1937 the Club was helping a school for girls and a crippled children's hospital. The Wilmette Homeowner's Association was organized to fight the spread of apartment buildings by restricting them to areas zoned for that purpose. The Association's 18-member board, comprised of residents from different Village sections, began to study taxes, zoning, and other problems affecting the homeowner.

In August, 1932, Wilmette schools again found themselves in a financial crisis, without funds to reopen in the fall. The *Wilmette Life* for August 25 asked parents of school children to loan the schools $10 per month per child for the coming nine-month school year, so schools could open on September 19. By mid-September, nearly $30,000 had been raised, enough to open the schools and guarantee their operation for at least half the year.

In spite of the pressing financial problems, Wilmette residents found time to be concerned about the deteriorating level of local politics. In May, 1932, after a particularly bitter pre-election campaign, a group of residents met and organized the Harmony Convention, electing Hoyt King chairman. Destined to be active for nearly 40 years, the organization pledged to eliminate "factional strife" from Village elections by nominating qualified, independent Wilmette people to community positions. The *Wilmette Life* for May 5 endorsed the Harmony Convention, commenting, "If the time and energy expended in fighting against each other were expended in fighting *with* each other for the good of the Village as a whole, the whole mental attitude of Wilmette would be changed within a year." In an early attempt at democratic selection, the Creative Committee was organized of two or more members of major Village organizations, including the American Legion, Chamber of Commerce, League of Women Voters, Woman's Club, Church Federation, Optimists, and Rotary. This Committee selected delegates to the Harmony Convention, representatives being selected from each precinct. These delegates nominated candidates for approval of the entire Convention. Candidates were selected for Village, Park and Library Boards, but the school board election remained independent and uninfluenced by the Harmony caucus plan.

Anti-Saloon Window Poster, 1933 or 1934. Opponents of liquor sales in unincorporated No Man's Land were urged to support the ballot proposal which would have prohibited retail liquor sales in area of New Trier Township not within corporate limits of the communities. Prohibition, which had eliminated the problem, had been repealed.

If you wish to

Keep Saloons
out of
New Trier Township
Vote YES
on Ballot

Shall the sale at retail of alcoholic liquor be prohibited in that part of New Trier Township lying without the corporate limits of any city, village or incorporated town in said Township?	YES	X
	NO	

Tuesday, April 10th

(Please Paste This Sheet in Your Window)

When a full slate of candidates had been chosen, the Harmony Convention submitted its candidates to the voters. Interestingly, in the first election the Harmony Convention was defeated when incumbent President Carbon P. Dubbs was re-elected after support in a closed caucus, defeating the Harmony slate. But the Harmony candidates won the next election in 1934 and, for years, took most of the positions unopposed.

On the sub-zero night of March 8, 1932, one of the North Shore's most spectacular fires destroyed the two-story Miralago on Sheridan Road in No Man's Land.

Run on Wilmette State Bank, 1932. Confidence and calmness on the part of bank officials prevented a heavy withdrawal of deposits by customers and bank closing, and brought back most of the deposits within a few days after the Saturday, June 23 "run."

Miralago Ballroom, 1929. Designed by architect George Fred Keck, the ballroom at No Man's Land included ten shops and the l,200 capacity ballroom on the second floor. In 1929, *Western Architect* described the design as "ship-like, a sea-breeze building" and described the silver leaf ceilings, and lobby neon tube fountain, saying that the project was "A roadhouse on the lake, catering to the young set of automobiling, jazz-dancing nite lifers." Photographs courtesy George Fred Keck.

The fire was discovered at 4:45 p.m. and the alarm was sounded. But the previous fall, Wilmette had withdrawn fire protection for the area and shut off the water supply, when No Man's Land property owners refused the Village offer to furnish water to fight fires for $500 a month, payable in advance.

When Wilmette and Winnetka did not respond to the alarm, the Evanston fire department came immediately, tapping a Kenilworth hydrant. Just as the fire was almost under control, Kenilworth police shut off the hydrant, because the Miralago had no contract with that suburb for water to fight fires. Kenilworth village clerk Wendell H. Clark ordered the water turned back on at 6 p.m., and Wilmette President Dubbs ordered Village firemen to help Evanston battle the blaze. At midnight, Winnetka firemen joined the two communities. But the flames were fanned by a brisk northwest wind, and the Miralago was largely destroyed, with damage set at $80,000. Suits totaling $250,000 filed against Kenilworth by the Miralago company and the building owners were dismissed by the Superior Court, and Kenilworth was judged not guilty. The court decision was certainly influenced by the complaints about No Man's Land, an unincorporated strip of gasoline stations, hot dog and barbecue stands, tacky buildings where fireworks banned in Wilmette were sold, and where syndicate gambling and slot machines went under cover when investigators came around.

Wilmette had long considered annexation as the best solution, and in September, 1936, residents held a mass meeting with Kenilworth citizens to protest a plan which would make No Man's Land a separate village. In June, 1939, the Illinois legislature passed a bill permitting Wilmette or Kenilworth to annex the area,

and the following month amended the bill to specify only Wilmette. But before Wilmette could complete the steps necessary for the annexation, the Illinois Supreme court voided the statute when Stanley K. Gage, the principal landowner in the area, instituted legal proceedings to curb Wilmette's annexation move.

But annexation was inevitable, and in 1941 Illinois allowed Wilmette to annex No Man's Land without a town vote. On January 6, 1942, a month after Pearl Harbor, Wilmette's board of trustees voted to annex the area. Although No Man's Land (as the area continued to be called for many years) was now a part of Wilmette, the zoning code prevented making improvements to the non-conforming properties and the appearance of the area continued to bring complaints.

In 1932, tension created by the contuing seriousness of the economy brought a short-lived run by depositors on the Wilmette State Bank. When the First National Bank of Evanston closed its doors on Saturday, June 25, and was in the hands of the national banking examiners, the news traveled like lightning. That day, depositors of the Wilmette State Bank formed a long line to withdraw their money. At noon, bank president Judson F. Stone told the waiting customers that the bank had ample cash, after which most of the crowd left, with greater confidence. The bank remained open all afternoon and evening, and many Wilmette residents who had withdrawn their money returned to reopen their accounts. The following week, in a *Life* advertisement, the bank thanked depositors for their support and solicited new depositors to open accounts with complete confidence.

Although Wilmette's bank remained solvent and open, many residents lost their jobs as conditions

Aerial View of Central Wilmette, April, 1931. The historic Andrew Sherman home at lower center still stood, the site of the Illinois Bell office on 12th Street was a sandlot baseball diamond, the North Shore Line tracks ran just west of the old Village Hall, and there seemed to be more open space around the central business district.

worsened. In mid-July, 1932, President Dubbs asked working residents to support the man-a-block plan, to "soften the blows of adversity that are landing so heavily upon so many of our worthy fellow citizens." The plan asked residents of each block or two blocks to provide at least one hour's work a week at 50 cents an hour for the 600 unemployed who had registered at Village Hall.

President Dubbs predicted that Wilmette's jobless would increase to 3,000 as winter approached, and said that members of a Committee on Unemployment would canvass the Village, contacting every household to try to get commitments of five days of work a week for everyone, and wages of $10 to $30 a week. Work would include repairs, lawn tending, cleaning, and other odd jobs. In the first week, 280 hours had been pledged, but the *Wilmette Life* observed that only 218 of 3,000 housholds had offered work. For weeks, the Committee urged support in articles, noting that a former bank president was now a clerk earning $22.50 a week, and a salesman who had earned several thousand dollars a year now worked in a factory for 40 cents an hour. "These men and women DO NOT WANT CHARITY — they DO want WORK," said the Committee. As more residents offered jobs, the worst depths of unemployment slowly began to ease, although conditions remained serious until the last few years of the decade.

Wilmette residents in August, 1934, were forgetting their cares by seeing one or more Wilmette Theater films, including James Cagney and Joan Blondell in "He Was Her Man;" Janet Gaynor and Charles Farrell in "Change of Heart;" James Gleason and Edna May Oliver in "Murder on the Blackbarrel," and William Powell in "The Key." Admission was 25 cents for adults, 10 cents for children. The Wilmette Ice Company advertised its stock of Pabst Blue Ribbon beer and ale, and the San Pedro Restaurant in No Man's Land enticed patrons by advertising, "Air cooled by Frigidaire," and that luncheons were 35 cents to 60 cents, dinners 65 cents to $1.10. That spring, Wilmette put its $520,000 waterworks into operation, and four years later began supplying Glenview with water.

On Saturday, November 30, 1935, the new Wilmette post office held open house for residents, with postmaster Herbert L. O'Connell on hand for the flag-raising ceremonies. On the previous April 30, Miss Jennie Shantz retired from the post office after 35 years of service which had begun in May, 1900, when the Wilmette post office was housed in a small one-story building opposite the Chicago & North Western depot. She recalled that the postmaster was Sam S. Dingee, her cousin, and that Edwin Drury succeeded him. There was no delivery, so patrons had to come to the post office for their mail until delivery was started in 1905. Perhaps her long service was an inheritance from her grandfather, pioneer settler Amos Shantz, who served as Village president from 1875-1878.

Wilmette's Shawnee Country Club faced financial collapse in 1935, with bills ahead of resources, until 55 Club members raised $15,250 to keep the landmark institution operating. Originally founded in 1897 as the Ouilmette Country Club, located in the deep woods at Ninth Street and Ashland Avenue, the club's name was changed to Shawnee in 1927, when the Ouilmette Country Club and the Century Club of Evanston were consolidated. The structure at Lake and Michigan was completed and dedicated in March, 1929, at a cost of $398,000. In January, 1943, the name again was changed to Michigan Shores Country Club.

Park expansion was temporarily satisfied in December, 1937, when the Park District board bought three properties on the lake front north of Washington Avenue for $100,000, to expand the beach area from the harbor to Forest Avenue. Private development was reported in the *Chicago Daily News* for November 12, 1938, when builder and developer Irwin A. Blietz acquired an eight-acre tract between Greenwood Avenue and Kenilworth. The land was purchased from Lloyd G. Gage, whose family had held the tract since 1894. Blietz announced plans to build 44 authentic colonial-style homes in a village atmosphere, to sell from $11,500 to $25,000. Home prices included landscaping and improvements, and prospective residents were to be screened by an advisory board including Blietz and residents of the colonial community, which was to be completed by the following May.

The Gage name made headlines again the following year, when the first floor of the Gage Mansion at Chestnut Avenue and Sheridan Road, was the scene of an elaborate Gay Nineties costume party given by Mr. and Mrs. Arthur H. Witzleben of Kenilworth. The *Wilmette Life* for November 30, 1939, reported that the home contained 18 rooms, high ceilings, parquet floors, and a parlor with two wood-burning fireplaces, and that a prize would be given to the couple wearing the best costumes.

In 1940, Wilmette's population had increased to 17,226, from 15,233 in the 1930 census and 7,814 in 1920. In April, 20 founders of the Lions Club of Wilmette held a charter night dinner in the Masonic Temple, at which Martin L. Olson presided. The

Wilmette Life, April, 1941.

Chief Zibble (center)
and Wilmette's Regular
Fire-Fighting Personnel,
1941. (Wilmette Life photo)

Chief McGuire (in
mufti) and Wilmette's
Police Department, 1941.
(from the Wilmette Life)

following February, voters approved $156,000 for a new public school west of Ridge Road, and the J. Robb Harper school was soon completed, named after the superintendent. It was the last school to be constructed during World War II, but the rapid western development of the Village was a spur to more school building in the postwar years.

On October 16, 1940, peacetime registration for military conscription began under the Selective Service Act. New Trier township men 21 to 35 registered, creating lists from which some men were to be chosen for a year's service. War clouds were gathering in August, 1941, when the Village supported the National

Largest Draft Contingent Leaves Wilmette For Training Centers, 1941. This picture, taken by Police Officer Edwin F. Whiteside, in the June 26, 1941, issue of the *Wilmette Life* shows a group of forty men who left Wilmette earlier in the month for induction into America's defense army. The caption did not identify individuals, but mentioned that 11 were volunteers, the balance having been drafted by the local Selective Service Board No. 2, which included Wilmette, Kenilworth, and a part of Glenview.

Defense effort by holding an aluminum drive and, with strong community cooperation, built an "aluminum mountain." At the drive's end on August 10, Boy Scouts led a parade, the music furnished by the clanging of aluminum pots and pans. They were met by David C. Leach, chairman of Wilmette's Council of Defense, at the rally point near Wilmette and Central Avenues, site of the "mountain."

Village President Harry C. Kinne had won a third term in April, 1941, defeating his opponent Henry J. Brandt by 2,321 to 1,673. At the mid-year point in 1941, the *Wilmette Life* published an article which touched on some of the "serious civic problems," including political cleavages, three park authorities, and three school bodies with different outlooks, the "commercial threat from No Man's Land," and the "large number of bootleg apartments." Stated positively, the article said what was needed were a new library building, better communication between elected Village officials and the public, strict collection of delinquent taxes, a program to teach school children about local problems, and a professional village manager for the board, free of worry over re-election, who could help the volunteer board members.

Almost on the eve of Pearl Harbor, the November 20th *Wilmette Life* advertised a 1942 Packard 6 Sedan for $695 and a 1941 Plymouth wagon for $950. One east Wilmette home on a 50x200 foot lot with four

1941 Advertisement.

bedrooms and porch was advertised for $9,000, and with Christmas a month away, Bernie's Studios offered three 5x7 photographs for $6.50. A 1942 model RCA Victor radio was $490, and the post office expected the heaviest Christmas load in years. Former newsman James R. Young was to speak locally on Japan, ironically, and North Shore architects talked about low-cost defense housing in the $6,000 price range. The Teatro del Lago theater was showing "Citizen Kane," starring Orson Welles, to capacity audiences.

On December 7, 1941, Japan attacked Pearl Harbor and World War II began for the nation and for Wilmette. The Wilmette Civilian Defense Council called an emergency meeting December 11 in the Village Hall, to plan a program of citizens defense with the American Legion. In the early weeks of the war, the Village took steps to guard against possible sabotage by floodlighting the beach and water plant, and the Legion Post 46 set up 16 areas with a captain for each, to mobilize civilians quickly should a disaster occur. William C. Reinhold of the Wilmette Council of Defense warned in the December 25 *Life* banner story that "it can happen here," urging everyone "from Boy Scout and Girl Scout age to 75" to be prepared to help in the event of an attack on American soil.

As the first month of the war ended, No Man's Land was finally annexed to the Village, and trustees prepared to remove the area's large billboards and to begin inspections for fire and health hazards. Merchants like Ace Motor Sales at 435 Green Bay Road advertised their commitment to the war effort, the Ace employees announcing in January, 1942, that they were sacrificing their new car business and "would rather see planes and tanks and Jeeps roll off the Ford production lines than new cars for us to sell." Wilmette residents were jolted by films of the December, 1940, London fire-bombings shown by the Defense Council, which had started a recreation and physical fitness program to strengthen both bodies and morale. Local Draft Board No. 2 at 1137 Central Avenue readied itself to register 2,000 men from Wilmette, Kenilworth and Glenview for military service.

Space is too limited for the complete story of the Village during World War II. A few of the highlights of those years should be mentioned, however. In March, 1942, the *Wilmette Life* reported the plan for sugar rationing, with a "probable allotment of either one

Map of Wilmette, Circa 1944.
As World War II was ending,
Wilmette's population was
about 17,500. the North
Shore line operated along
Greenleaf Avenue, Edens
Expressway had not been
built, and much of the
western section had not been
subdivided. Map drawn by
Village Manager William A.
Wolff, and published in
Wilmette Handbook, issued
circa 1948.

MAP OF VILLAGE OF W

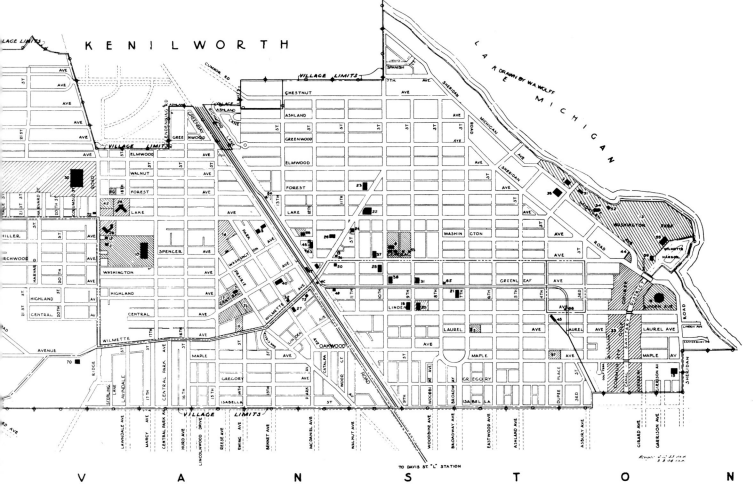

Wilmette World War II Scrap Drive, 1942. Former fire marshal Walter Zibble stands by a typical collection, from rubber tires, old hose and metal barrels to car wheels and shelving.

Wilmette Life, March 27, 1941.

John Gooch Baby Is Named for Wilmette

Wilmette has many loyal sons and daughters but the title of the village's most ardent fan may well go to John W. Gooch, of Milwaukee, Wis., formerly of Wilmette.

On March 10 his wife, Mrs. Gooch, had a little boy, their first baby. Because Mr. Gooch lived here for a long time and has liked the village of Wilmette, the people, the schools, the atmosphere, in fact everything about the town the infant was named John Wilmette Gooch. To our knowledge, this is the first baby named in honor of the village.

Wilmette's (in spite of his aristocratic name he no doubt will be called "Willy") paternal grandmother is Mrs. Josephine Gooch of Wilmette, a resident here for many years, and his maternal grandparents are Mr. and Mrs. Thomas Halverson of Wausau, Wis.

pound per person every two weeks, or three-quarters of a pound every week." In September, the American Red Cross Blood Donor Service waged a five-day Wilmette campaign in the Woman's Club, and the Wilmette Civilian Defense Council announced that its monthly salvage drive had amassed more than 70 tons of tin cans, scrap metal, rags, rubber, newspapers, and magazines from stores and homes. To save gasoline, Village residents were urged in October to join the share-the-ride movement, before the national gasoline rationing program began the following month. Oil and gasoline rationing were in effect by late November, and by December, more than 1,000 Wilmette, Kenilworth and Glenview men were in active service. Rationing of coffee, sugar, and fuel oil on a point basis began in January, 1943. Car owners were rated as A, B, or C, the A coupon book good for 240 miles a month, the B book for 400 miles, and the C book with no limit, for defense workers, doctors, driving for the war effort, servicemen and others involved in essential war work. There were air raid drills, starting in May, 1943, in which Village residents simulated steps to be taken.

A more welcome activity was Wilmette's Service Men's Center at 403 Linden Avenue, which a *Life* article in the October 21, 1943, issue described as furnished with a piano, radio, phonograph, pool tables, pingpong tables and writing desks, when the Center opened four days earlier. For the next few war years, there were dances, lists of Village rooms for rent to servicemen's wives and relatives, and coffee and sandwiches from a kitchen near the library books and magazines. School children in Wilmette and in New Trier High School saved money for war stamps and bonds, and rode trucks on Saturdays to collect scrap metal and papers. The author recalls as a New Trier student during the war that boys ran a commando course which included scaling walls, sprinting, distance running, and hurdling, with low times posted. Gasoline was rationed, as were tires, meat, sugar, chocolate, butter, and a variety of foods earmarked for men in service and allied countries.

With the end of World War II in August, 1945, Wilmette moved to develop a new plan for improvements curbed by wartime shortages. The 1946 Village Plan submitted by the Wilmette Planning Board under chairman Lloyd D. Miller proposed to spend $3,785,000, the total including a new school for Central and Logan, a fire station for western Wilmette, an addition to the Green Bay fire station to house police and add a jail, a new library, a remodeled Village Hall, and four additional parks.

One of the Plan's major projects was a War Memorial Community Center, in the middle of a block bounded by Green Bay, Wilmette, Park and Central, which would be cleared of existing private homes and would include the new library on the southwest corner. Within a few years, all the Plan proposals were accepted and implemented, except for the War Memorial Center, the Village Hall remodeling, and part of the park land acquisitions.

The bowl in Washington Park was constructed as a W.P.A. project in 1938-39, and was designed by Gordon Wallace, Superintendent of Parks from 1937 to 1968. Concerts in the bowl were an early tradition; in the early years many performances were given by the W.P.A. Concert Orchestra. In July, 1946, the stage of the Washington Park bowl was dedicated, the $10,000 gift of Charles H. Feltman, a park district commissioner since 1937. Mr. Wallace, for whom the bowl was named after his retirement in 1968, is now a resident of Tomah, Wisconsin, and recalls the two-year construction project as a particularly satisfying one, as does F. Cushing Smith, former park commissioner, who offered advice and planning assistance.

On Valentine's Day in 1948, Wilmette voters went to the polls to vote upon 18 civic improvement proposals which, if approved, would add 15% to their tax bills. The result of nearly four years of planning by the Wilmette Planning Board, the Referendum offered the voters the opportunity to approve school modernization, a new library, park and village improvements, a War Memorial Community Building, and extension of water and sewer mains into largely vacant and tax delinquent southwestern Wilmette.

Of the 18 proposals the voters, in unprecedented numbers, chose those they wanted most and were willing to pay for. Of unusual significance was approval of the southwestern extension of water and sewer mains, evidencing unselfish civic support. This project made possible orderly development and the return to the tax rolls of this significant area. The voters rejected a Community Building.

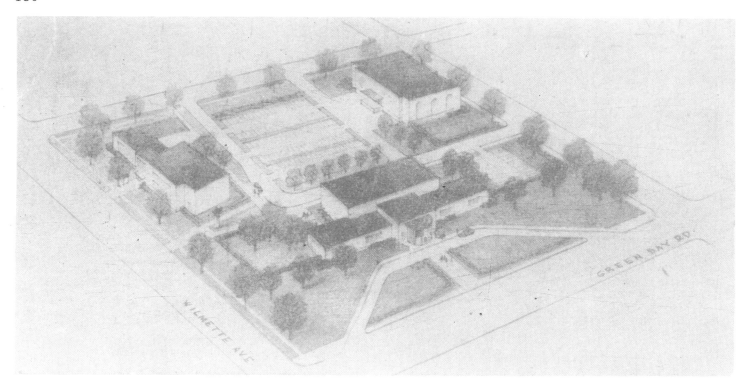

Sketch of Proposed War Memorial Center, 1948. This drawing appeared in the *Chicago Daily News* for January 30, 1948. The sketch shows the Community House at center, post office, upper right, and library, left.

Wilmette observed its 75th anniversary in 1947, with a celebration steering committee headed by W. B. (Bal) Robinson, Jr. One of the most tangible products was the 120-page special 75th anniversary issue published by the *Wilmette Life*, including articles, profiles of pioneers, photographs and maps, covering institutions, commercial ventures, leading citizens, and development of the Village from its earliest days. Events included the Woman's Club art exhibit, a historic artifacts display, and a special session of Ye Olde Towne Folkes with skits and old-fashioned clothes. The big celebration ran from May 28 to June 12, highlighted by the May 31 all-Village party at the Michigan Shores Club and sports events on July 4. During the year, there were open houses in public buildings, a pageant by school children, church services, a New Trier band concert, and publication of a guidebook, "The Story of Wilmette, As Told in Books," by the Library.

Wilmette Historian Dedicates Trail Tree Plaque, 1949. Herbert B. Mulford is shown addressing a group of Cub Scouts and Boy Scouts attending the late fall dedication of the plaque marking the trail tree at 10th & Greenwood.

In September, 1949, the Village board established the Wilmette Historical Commission, providing for a chairman and eight members to be appointed annually by the board and president for one-year terms. Primary purposes of the new commission were to collect and preserve historical objects, explore matters of historical significance, and to obtain financial support. Terms of office for commission members were changed to staggered terms. The following May, Village President William H. Alexander and the board appointed Horace Holley chairman, and as members, Mrs. William H.

Alexander, Miss Jean Drucker, John M. Eckert, Leon R. Steffens, Mrs. John C. Ogren, and Bailey Shearer. For their work in collecting and preserving Wilmette historical data, James D. W. Kline and Herbert B. Mulford were named honorary commission members. A temporary museum was soon installed in the basement of Village Hall.

With a solid foundation for Wilmette's historical efforts established, the Village moved toward the 1950's with much accomplished, but much still to be done.

Mallinckrodt College, Aerial View, 1930's.
Mallinckrodt College is the outgrowth of
a normal school, established by the Sisters
of Christian Charity in the 1870's in
Pennsylvania. The present building was
built during World War I, shortly
after the order was transferred to
Wilmette. Since 1961 the college
has been a two-year liberal arts college,
recently expanding to evening programs.

10
Modern Times: 1950-1976

Ruins of the Vista del Lago, May, 1962. High rise buildings are under construction in the background. Ruins of the private club were visible for many years after Wilmette annexed No Man's Land in 1942.

Wilmette's first 75 years were a period of physical growth, population expansion, and development of the institutions which a community, large or small, must have to survive and prosper. From a handful of houses in the thick woods where the trains from Chicago and the north stopped only infrequently, the Village had become an upper middle-class suburb, part of the wealthiest congressional district in the nation. Most of its residents earned their living in Chicago, but they were concerned about Wilmette, about education, the quality of services, and the existence, or non-existence, of effective community institutions.

Although the community had experienced periods of rapid growth in previous decades, the growth of the 1950's and 1960's was unprecedented. The population in 1940 was 17,226, double that of 1920 largely due to absorbing the Village of Gross Point. Some unique combination of geography, transportation, and municipal services attracted many newcomers, and the population rose from 18,162 in 1950 to 28,268 in 1960, reaching 32,000 in 1966. One remarkable consequence of the post-war population explosion was that the income and educational level of the newcomers equalled, and then exceeded those of previous census reports on the Village.

In 1948, Edens Expressway was under construction, linking west Wilmette with Chicago's center, and providing a major impetus to the residential development of Wilmette's western neighborhoods. Carson Pirie Scott & Company completed their new suburban shopping center, Edens Plaza, with Old

Edens Plaza, Under Construction, 1956. The successful shopping center at Lake and Skokie has had additions since the first building, and later became the home of Wilmette's third bank, Edens Plaza State Bank.

Orchard, provided a magnet which the western areas had not previously seen. Wilmette historian Herbert B. Mulford expressed a contemporary view of the population explosion in 1956, in his pamphlet *Wilmette and the Suburban Whirl:*

"Most dramatic were the physical changes by which corn, pumpkin and cabbage fields of pioneer truck gardeners almost overnight became a landscape of roof tops. Month on month trucks, bulldozers and concrete-mixers cleared land, dug ditches, and made foundations, to be followed by hordes of other construction workers employed by scores of organizations speculating on the demand for housing . . .

"Numerous other signs of the times should have made residents conscious of the significance of the expansion. The Village government had to ration water for both Glenview and Wilmette users pending doubling the waterworks facilities. The collection of fees for new building permits reached almost $100,000 a year and made a very considerable item in the Village budget. . ."

The modern Village period began with an important new structure, when the new public library was completed in 1950. Called "one of the Village's best assets" in the 1973 Comprehensive Plan, the new library expanded over two decades under the guidance of Helen J. Siniff. A junior room was established in 1959, a new children's wing in 1965, and expanded reference rooms in 1967. The very popular fine arts section was completed in 1970. The library has one of the highest circulation rates in Illinois for towns of the size, and by 1975 the collection totalled 130,000 volumes. In 1974 Richard Thompson joined the library as the new director, and under his leadership, the library's programs in the community have been expanded.

The population increases of the 1950's and 1960's placed enormous demands on the Village's school systems, which experienced intense growth during the period. Most of Wilmette is served by District 39, and the school population it serves jumped from 2,000 students in 1950, to 5,200 in 1970. Prior to the administration of long-time superintendent Millard D. Bell, the old Gross Point School District 40 was merged into Wilmette's District 39, adding the Highcrest School, which was built in the 1920's. Mr. Bell's years from 1942 to 1965 saw the establishment of the junior high school system, and the addition of new grade schools for sections west of Ridge Road. In 1941, Harper School was built to serve the recently developed Kenilworth Gardens and Indian Hill Estates areas. The new Logan School was completed in 1947, and a new Central School built in 1949-50, but more expansion was necessary in 1962. Romona School was built in 1957-58, amply provided with open space, its ten acre site being the largest school site in the Village. Locust Junior High School was built

in 1961-62, as the school population in newly developed western neighborhoods continued its upward spiral. Howard Junior High School, originally built in 1927, was expanded in the 30's, then again in 1959 and 1968. Millard D. Bell School is the most recent (1964-65), named for the superintendent, who retired shortly before it was opened. Serving children in the southwest corner of the Village, Bell School opened as the school population edged toward its peak of 5200 students.

Commenting on the expansion of the schools as it was happening, Herbert H. Mulford wrote in 1956:

"It was striking that Wilmette children and youth were receiving education from three public school systems, two Roman Catholic parochial schools and a high school, one college laboratory school and at least two popular private schools. Broadly, the public schools served about twice as many pupils as the parochial schools.

"Roman Catholic parochial schools felt the population pressure also. On the far eastern side of the village St. Francis Xavier school added an assembly room and gymnasium, then added more classrooms. In the far western area Loyola Academy erected its new building. Land was acquired for Regina Dominican Convent and High School, which required new zoning action by the Village."

By the early 1960's it was evident that New Trier High School must be expanded to educate the post-World War II "baby boom" which had swelled the teen-age population. The township population had increased 42% between 1950 and 1960, and although a township referendum to build a second high school failed in 1962, in March, 1963, voters approved construction of the second high school in Northfield, to be called New Trier West. A long period of study and discussion led to decisions which placed students who lived in western neighborhoods, for the most part, at New Trier West, and those east at the old New Trier East.

Elementary schools continued to feel pressure from an expanding younger population in Wilmette during the 1960's, and in 1968 voters approved a $2 million bond issue for additions to Howard Junior High School and Locust and Logan Schools. In 1967, Donald V. Grote became superintendent of District 39, and although his stay in the school system spanned only four years, it was under his leadership, and the school board chaired by Oliver Townsend, that District 39 met the difficult challenges of the expanding school population of the late 1960's.

The inflation and economic boom of the late 60's and early 70's boosted real estate prices considerably, to the extent that by the early seventies, fewer young families were able to afford to become homeowners. The national trend toward smaller families was felt when the school population began to decline in 1972. As he assumed the superintendent's responsibilities in late 1974, Larry Love, who had served the district for nearly ten years, found the district needing to reverse direction and plan for fewer children and a declining income with which to educate them. Many west side classrooms were vacant by 1975, and the school district, under the leadership of Superintendent Love and school board chairman Harry Baumann, began to study how the board could best continue to reduce operating costs without sacrificing the quality education program Wilmette parents had come to expect.

Local elections were largely uneventful in the period following World War II, and the Board of Trustees, Park Board and Library Board continued to be occupied by candidates chosen by the caucus system. But in 1948 the Harmony caucus candidates were opposed by a full slate of Citizens Party nominees. It was a bitter election fight, and the vote tally on election night showed the challenging Citizens Party the winners, with the exception of incumbent Village president William H. Alexander, who was re-elected. The Citizens Party candidate for Village president, Earl Orner, sought a recount of the votes for that office in the county courts, but his suit resulted in a court-ordered recount of every contest. The recount resulted in his party losing all the seats they had won in the first count, due to irregularities.

In the next two decades, Harmony caucus candidates for local office were elected without opposition, and the community seemed to accept the caucus theme, "the office seeks the man." But in 1969, the Harmony caucus was split when some caucus delegates and supporters withdrew and formed an opposition party to the caucus slate, calling their new group of candidates the United Party.

The voters thought the election was resolved on the second Tuesday of April, 1969, with the election of former trustee James A. Schwietert, United Party candidate for Village president, and all other United Party candidates for trustee. Park and library board candidates did not run with party affiliation, but all those elected, with one exception, had been endorsed by the United Party. There was a heavy turnout of voters at the six polling places in the schools, and long lines necessitated waiting over two hours to vote at some locations. Some voters claimed they were unable

190

High Rise Apartment Under Construction, No Man's Land, 1962. Staircase and unfinished foundation of The Breakers is in foreground of this May, 1962, photograph.

to vote when the polls closed with people still standing in line outside.

Several residents who had been unable to vote filed suits in both state and federal courts, charging that the voters had been disenfranchised by the long wait and few polling places. One suit was successful, and a new election was ordered the following November, with 34 polling places open. Over 12,000 voters participated the first Tuesday in November; the result was essentially the same. The United Party winners again won, James A. Schwietert defeating Harmony caucus candidate Harold V. Webb for the village presidency.

In 1971, only three candidates filed for the three trustee openings, and all were mutually endorsed by the United Party and former Harmony caucus supporters. In 1972, the Wilmette Forum was organized to provide non-partisan campaign opportunities for candidates to meet the voters and discuss the issues of concern to both. In the 1973 election campaign, a full slate of candidates was entered by the Village Party and by the 1973 United Party. A number of independent candidates also ran for Village Board positions, and overall, 27 candidates were running for 14 openings.

The Forum created a Code of Fair Campaign Practices, which each of the 1973 candidates endorsed, monitored fair practices, and sponsored many meetings during the election period to provide an opportunity for all candidates to meet the public. Editorials on the subject in the *Wilmette Life* pointed to the Forum's activity as "insuring that an election campaign can be conducted without great expense and in an atmosphere where viewpoints can be expressed thoroughly."

The major issue of the campaign was the Board of Trustees' plan to construct a new Village Hall and train station without voter referendum. The project, financed by bonds issued under home rule powers granted to the Village under the state's new constitution, had been in the planning stages several years. Challenging Village Party candidates charged the issue should have been put to a referendum. There was a heavy voter turnout (6,237 votes cast), and the incumbent United Party candidates were replaced in office by independent and Village Party candidates; one non-incumbent United Party candidate was elected. By the time the election results were counted, the final documents for the project had been completed, and the building program proceeded.

During the balance of 1973, the Village Board devoted much time to discussion and consideration of the proposed new Village Hall. The modern center for Wilmette government was to be a 39,750 square-foot building on the site of the 1910 Hall, with parking extending across the 1897 Chicago and North Western depot area, necessitating a new railroad station to the north, a recommendation contained in the recently completed Comprehensive Plan. The relocation of the station caused the closing of a long-established Wilmette business, Hoffman Brothers Lumber Company, which found new quarters in Gurnee.

In early 1974, Village Manager Lund announced his retirement, having served nearly 10 years in the post. The Village board conducted an extensive search for his replacement, appointing Stan Kennedy to the position in summer of 1974.

In late 1973, Wilmette citizens rallied to the cause of historic preservation, when the Wilmette Historical Society opened a village-wide campaign to "Save-the-Depot," the 1873 brick depot used for years

as a freight building. The little depot on the west side of the tracks would be in the path of an access to the proposed new station, and through the efforts of the Society's directors and president Joanne Andrews, the North Western donated the structure to the Society on the condition that it be moved. Supporting the project, Wilmette's trustees made the west side of the municipal parking lot at 1135 Wilmette Avenue available as the relocation site. The Society raised an initial $15,000 to move the structure and excavate a basement, with key support by the *Wilmette Life*. On June 13, 1974, the contractors' men and trucks eased the sturdy 120,000 pound building down the embankment onto Green Bay Road, and as crowds of thousands

Moving the Depot, 1974. Loaded aboard the flatbed dolly, riding on steel beams, the 60-ton 1873 Depot waits at Wilmette and Green Bay for the northbound 7:04 train to pass before proceeding over the tracks to its new location.

watched in person and on Channel 2 TV News, the depot was transported over the tracks, down Wilmette Avenue, and maneuvered into position on the lot, to be moved forward to its permanent site when the foundation was completed that fall. Subsequently, the building was listed on the National Register of Historic Places, national recognition of the significant role played by the small building in the early pioneer years of the community. With assistance of grants from the Illinois Bicentennial Commission and the National Park Service, the Historical Society is completing remodeling which will allow commercial use of the building, income going to support the historical effort.

The Historical Society's active role in the community began in the late 1960's, following its founding in late 1965. First president was James A. Williams, and early officers Maynard Hazen, James V. Sill, and Elizabeth F. Kinnear led early efforts as the organization supplemented the work of the Wilmette Historical Commission.

Another organization new to the community in the 1960's is the Wilmette Jaycees, founded in the late 1950's. Active in many civic ventures, the Jaycees have conducted an annual opinion survey for over a decade, one which is highly accurate due to the large sample, and which measures public opinion on local services and new programs in the community. Results of the Jaycees survey are carefully studied by elected officials as they consider new programs and current issues.

One issue which faced the newly-elected Board of Trustees in the spring and summer of 1973 was the proposal to change the Village's century-old ban on the sale of alcoholic beverages. The Jaycees survey that spring indicated a majority of Village residents would

Recreation Explosion of the Late 60's and Early 70's.
Shown at far left is the Centennial Park complex
entrance, opened in 1972; at upper right is the
pool, center right Community Building, and bottom
right, Beach House, all completed in 1972. Upper
left shows the ice facility, completed later. In the
picture, near left, are Charlotte Atkinson and Mary
Buzzard, curling in the Curtis Curling Center.
(Photos courtesy Mary Buzzard and Coder Taylor)

not object to liquor sales, and that summer, Village president Warren Burmeister appointed a special commission to study the matter. The special commission solicited comments and testimony from village organizations, churches and residents, and reported to president Burmeister on their findings and on various alternatives which the Village might consider to change the existing laws. The trustees placed the subject on the ballot in March, 1974, in an advisory referendum at the time of the RTA referendum, and voters indicated they approved of the sale of liquor with meals in restaurants and also approved of allowing the sale of packaged liquor. Following the advisory referendum, the Board of Trustees passed the necessary ordinances to allow liquor to be sold.

During the decades following World War II, the Recreation Board, which was appointed by the Village trustees, was largely responsible for public recreation. It was not until 1945 that the park district extended west beyond Ridge Road, and through the fifties and sixties, although considerable land was acquired, the approach was one of passive recreation and physical park improvements. In August, 1955, the lakefront Washington Park was renamed Gillson Park, for long-time civic leader Louis K. Gillson, who had played so important a part in the development and growth of the Village park system.

The General Plan developed in 1952 by the Wilmette Planning Board forecast the ultimate population as 32,000, which was reached in the late 1960's. Their recommendations for acquisition of parks and playgrounds needed to service that size population have been met, and actually exceeded, by the Park District in the ensuing years.

As the population grew and demanded more and better programs, the park board began to make a dramatic shift in philosophy and emphasis, following a national trend to larger and better recreation programs in all parts of the country.

In 1961 the Park District retained the Recreation and Parks Field Service of the University of Illinois to appraise the community's facilities, which totaled 165 acres at the time, and most of the acquisitions over the next 10 years were the result of their recommendations In existence at that time were Gillson Park (1908), Vattman Park (1911), the Community Golf Course (1916), Forest Ave. Playground 926), Thornwood Park (1949-61), Maple Avenue Park (1949-63), Hibbard Park (1955-63), and Community Playfield (1954-64), which totals 39 acres, sharing recreational space with Highcrest School on the east, and Locust Junior High School on the west. In 1956-57, a portion of the former Sand-Lo Beach property was acquired, and re-named for former park commissioner Lawrence Langdon, to serve as the sailing beach. In 1961 West Park was acquired, and in 1964, Shorewood Park, our legacy from the abandoned North Shore Line tracks.

In 1968, the park board completed negotiations for the Loutsch property at Crawford, Old Glenview Road and Wilmette Avenue, the last remaining Gross Point farm. The agreement allowed the owner to continue living on his farm, and a later referendum saw the voters approve a sports complex of outdoor swimming pools and indoor tennis courts for the site. While Centennial Park was under construction, the park commissioners, under the leadership of Robert Gerrie, selected Ray VanDeWalle to be Director of Parks. The new park, which was developed around the Loutsch

No Man's Land, 1949. View north from Chestnut Street shows the string of shrimp, ice cream and gasoline structures which faced the lake and were the subject for much criticism from Wilmette residents and Village officials.

farmyard, was called Centennial Park, and completed in 1972.

In 1973, the Northwestern University Golf Course west of Edens Expressway was put up for sale, and residents urged the park board to purchase it to prevent apartment construction on the site and provide an 18-hole golf course for the community. The park board and new president William J. Lambrecht urged the voters to approve acquisition, and the May, 1973, referendum was successful.

In 1974, a number of interested residents asked the park board to enlarge the ice skating facilities, which then were limited to outdoor artificial ice formerly operated by the Recreation Department, by then absorbed into the Park District. After considerable study and public discussion, the park board decided to build a new $1,600,000 indoor ice facility at Centennial Park, which would be self-supporting by users' fees. It was the decision of the park board not to finance the ice rink with public funds; the sale of revenue bonds was considered, but the final decision was to obtain a long-term note, secured by the Park District's taxing

The Teatro del Lago, Circa
1946. Sam C. Meyers (far
right) and staff offered the
first Sunday movies in the
twenties and thirties, when
the area was still No Man's
Land. The theater was razed
in 1967 to build the Plaza del
Lago complex.

ability, not revenues from the structure. The new ice rink and two additional indoor tennis courts were completed in 1975, without referendum.

Another ice facility had been constructed nearly ten years before, on the Village Green on Ridge Road. The Curtis Curling Center, the nation's only public curling rink, had been the gift of Winnetka's curling enthusiast Darwin Curtis, and was given to the Village, which then operated recreation programs through the Recreation Board, under the Village board. Over the eight years since it opened, there have been continuing proposals to establish other uses for the building, due to difficulties in making the operation self-sustaining. In the early seventies, management of its programs was turned over to the Park District along with other recreation programs.

Adjacent to the curling facility is the Wilmette police headquarters, a new building which was completed in 1968 in the administration of Mayor Kenneth A. Santee. During his board's term, modernized water pumping and sewage facilities were added, the police headquarters was completed, but voters rejected a proposal to modernize the aging street light system, voting down a $2 million referendum proposal. The previous board, under the leadership of president Howard Decker, had successfully urged voters to approve the building of a new $174,000 fire station, immediately east of the C&NW tracks at Lake Avenue, on land formerly occupied by the North Shore Line tracks. One interesting decision of the trustees in 1965 was the controversial but far-sighted decision to stop using DDT spray to combat Dutch Elm disease.

Following the move to the new police headquarters,

space became available in the building on Green Bay Road known as the Village Hall Annex. Council Chambers, Police and Fire Departments once shared the building, but by the late 1960's, both the police and fire departments had new, larger quarters. The Recreation Board occupied the first floor of the building, and in 1969, The Wilmette Historical Museum was opened on the second floor. The two display rooms and office were the culmination of many years of work on the part of many residents, but particularly responsible were Jim Williams, Walter Cleave and Bal Robinson.

Armon Lund, Director of Public Works, had been appointed Village Manager that winter of 1964, succeeding William A. Wolff, who had served for 24 years. years. Early in Village Manager Lund's ten-year tenure, he urged construction of a new Village Hall, with the trustees in 1965 and 1966 inclined to either remodel or rebuild the 56-year-old structure on the same site.

Five years earlier, shortly after the election of Howard C. Decker as 1961-65 Village president, Decker took an important step by creating an informal planning council, comprised of the presidents of the various Village boards. By meeting jointly, each board knew the plans of the other organizations, and could coordinate and work co-operatively. It had been nearly 15 years since the Plan Board of the late 1940's had so successfully anticipated the growth that was to come, and new pressures now made planning essential to good government.

During the administration of the 29th Village president, Kenneth A. Santee (whose preference was for the term "Mayor"), the Board of Trustees moved decisively on the recommendations of the Planning Board established in the early sixties and established the Wilmette Plan Commission. The Village subsequently hired the professional planning firm of Carl Gardner & Associates to do a comprehensive study of the Village in terms of future needs and services, to guide the Board of Trustees toward development of a Comprehensive Plan for the Village. Nearly all of the land which had been vacant as recently as 1945 was by now occupied by residential developments or parks, and the direction of

Central Business District, Mini-Mall Illustrations from the Comprehensive Plan, 1971. These artist's sketches show the 1100 block of Central Avenue as it looked in 1970, and as it would look with remodelling of the buildings and implementation of the suggestions of the planners.

the future was to be conservation and management of the existing neighborhoods.

The Plan was developed with the guidance and advice of the Plan Commission, led first by Chairman R. Newton Rooks in 1967, and later Paul Gerden in 1968. Donald Newton became chairman in 1969, and he and the commission held extensive public hearings following the Gardner firm's preliminary background studies and recommendations. Included in the preliminary Plan were projections for educational needs based on a special census of school population, as well as projections of the effect of future land use decisions on the Village's tax base.

The major goals and objectives developed during the five-year professional study were that the Village should remain primarily residential, and that it should strive to enhance the humanitarian and aesthetic qualities of the community. Another objective was that adequate housing for families both young and old should be encouraged, emphasizing housing for senior

First Federal Savings, 1976.
Wilmette's second financial
institution was founded in
the 1930's, and during the
early years had offices on
Wilmette Avenue. The
present structure, at Green
Bay and Central, was built in
the fifties, and remodelled in
1974, as one of the
significant signs of renewal in
the central business district.

citizens, and for those who are employed within the
Village.

The Comprehensive Plan, amended somewhat from
the plan originally proposed, was adopted in 1973. A
new zoning ordinance was drafted in connection with
the recommendations in the Plan, and its adoption was
the work of the 1974 Board of Trustees.

During the 1960's, Wilmette joined other
communities across the nation to work towards fair
housing and equal opportunities for minorities.

The Board of Trustees passed a fair housing ordinance
considerably in advance of the federal laws, assuring
access to housing in Wilmette to everyone. Housing for
the elderly had been of concern to many church
and volunteer groups within the Village over the decade
from 1965-75, and the efforts of the Wilmette Council
for Elderly Housing and the League of Women Voters
led to adoption of a zoning classification for new
construction, which allows development of
housing which is specially designed for this

Plaza del Lago, 1975. The apartments and shops of the motor court were built as part of the original Spanish Court development, which in 1926 included the Teatro del Lago and Miralago Ballroom on the west side of Sheridan Road, and private clubs The Breakers and Vista del Lago on the lakeshore.

First National Bank, 1975.
Wilmette's fourth banking
institution, the 1st National
was built adjacent to the
Plaza del Lago shopping
complex, and occupies a
prominent site at the gateway
to Wilmette. It typifies the
striking changes which have
come to No Man's Land.

residential use. The new zoning classification has
allowed a new housing facility for the elderly to be built
on property adjacent to the Congregational Church,
with financing provided by federal programs.
Construction is scheduled to begin in fall, 1976.

Of continuing concern to the trustees of the
Village in the decade from 1965-75 was the decline of
the Village's shopping districts. With the exception of
the Plaza del Lago and Edens Plaza, competition from
new, large shopping centers and discount merchandising,
the Village's retail sales were not keeping pace with
residents' spending.

Nearly two decades after Wilmette had annexed
No Man's Land, the area's zoning categories were
changed in 1958, and construction began on the first of
the area's luxury cooperative highrises at 1410 Sheridan
Road. In October, 1965, the Spanish Court site and
buildings were sold to land developer Plato Foufas.
Foufas announced plans for a $4 million shopping
center, and construction soon began.

One of the casualties of this distinctly beneficial
project was the razing of the Teatro del Lago theater, to
provide space for parking and additions to the existing
shops. The theater had been a landmark for area
residents since it opened in April, 1927. Sadly, owner
Sam C. Meyers recalled that the theater had provided
jobs for actor Rock Hudson and U. S. Senator Charles
Percy in their boyhood days; opening in what he called
a "wilderness area", it had spanned the era from silent
films to talkies.

If the Plaza del Lago was a smashing success,
business in other commercial areas was not, and in the
early 1970's Wilmette's business districts faced
increasing competition. In 1974 the trustees created

the Council for Commercial Renewal, an all-volunteer council of retailers, property owners, consumers and other residents with special expertise, to work together to try to improve the quality and selection of goods and services in the central business district and other areas. The Council has made shopper surveys, parking studies, photographic surveys, and improvement recommendations to the Village board for appropriate action.

In 1975 there was brief community discussion of reviving the caucus system, but by the January filing date, 14 individuals had filed petitions for seats on the Village, Park and Library boards, and campaigned under the Forum's fair practices code. All those elected were independent candidates, although the United Party did organize a slate of candidates for the Village Board.

Wilmette residents became pioneers again in January, 1967, when a paralyzing snowstorm struck the Chicago area, dumping a record 30 inches on January 26 and 27. Traffic came to a halt for three days, people learned again how dependent they could be on on each other, and common sights were people skiing or snow-shoeing around town on essential errands. Village plows mounded snow into a gigantic mountain at Lake and Wilmette, which did not melt until late spring.

Community events have sprung up in various parts of town, and in 1966, residents of the 1400 block of Gregory Avenue held the first Gregory Street Fair, a neighborhood event which continues to be held in July each year. Another Wilmette annual event is the Fourth of July Parade held in west Wilmette, in the area of the old Gross Point farming community. Antique wagons and a picnic are featured, along with the latest

generation of the pioneer families, the Rengels, Engels and others. In 1970, the Fourth of July Committee was organized under the Recreation Department and began the first of the community celebrations held at Gillson Park, with Ed Barys as chairman. The annual Family Day traditionally concludes with a concert in the Wallace Bowl and fireworks over the lake.

The year 1972 was the Centennial year for the Village, and Wilmette's 100th anniversary was duly observed with a variety of events. During the year, 12 Wilmette citizens were honored with Outstanding Citizen Awards, one each month, for their leadership and civic contributions. Award recipients were Helen J. Siniff, Dr. Martin H. Seifert, James A. Williams, Jane Alexander, James P. Reichmann, Ralph Klinge, E. Todd Wheeler, Jeanne Bonynge, Stanley Hughey, Carl W. Vorreiter, Dr. Josephine Earlywine, and Harry L. Parsons.

Climax of the year-long celebration was the Centennial Fair held Sunday, September 24, featuring art and craft exhibits, antique exhibits, entertainment by local groups, and a street dance. Sponsored by the Wilmette Centennial Commission, chaired by Deborah Burdick and Lea Bohlman, the Fair was conceived and managed by Joanne Andrews. Attended by over 20,000 people, it was a very popular event with residents, and has been continued each year since 1972, renamed the Wilmette Community Fair.

Something new was added to Village services when in March, 1974, the trustees approved a 90-day trial period for Wilmette's own bus system, with four buses operating on three routes which linked the east side transportation centers with Edens Plaza, Old Orchard, and New Trier West, and connected with North

Centennial Fair, 1972. Top, right, Vic Bohlman, Nancy and Tom Bischoff get the cake ready for its debut on stage; below, the crowd on the lawn of Village Hall enjoying entertainment by the Alewives, Armstrong Family Folksingers, dixieland band, park district dancers, and Order of the Arrow Indian dancers. Master of Ceremonies was Walter Jacobson. (Wilmette Life photos)

The Wilmette Bank, 1974. Wilmette's first banking institution was founded in the last century. The new bank building, completed in 1972, is a totally modern building, the first new silhouette in the central business district in many years. (Courtesy Perkins & Will)

Lifetime Residents the Wheelers Give Wilmette A Park. In 1971, Mr. and Mrs. E. Todd Wheeler donated a 238 by 240 foot building lot on Catalpa Place to the Wilmette Park District, to be used for a tot-lot in the neighborhood. Mr. Wheeler, who was born in his home on adjacent Wood Court, donated the property in memory of his parents, Mr. and Mrs. C. A. Wheeler, who moved to Wilmette in 1895. The picture at right shows the property before the house was razed and park improvements were made in 1973. The finished product, Wheeler Park, is shown below.

Mr. Wheeler, an architect and former member of the Wilmette Plan Commission, retired in 1972 and enjoys, with Mrs. Wheeler, watching the neighborhood children using the park, something they both felt had been needed in the area for years. Lora Wheeler, a former member of the Recreation Board and former president of the League of Women Voters, said at the time of the land donation that she and her husband had bought the additional land in the 1950's with the intention of donating it, because "the children needed it." (Courtesy *Wilmette Life*)

C&NW RR Depot, 1976
Opened in the summer of
1975, the station
compliments the new
look of the central
business district.
(Courtesy Coder Taylor)

Suburban Transit District service outside the village limits. The system proved successful from the beginning, a large portion of that success being due to the energetic young drivers and managers of the company which provides the service, who are known for their extraordinary service and courtesy.

In early September, 1975, Wilmette's new railroad depot opened to commuters, the fourth C&NW railroad structure in the Village's history, counting the first wooden depot which burned before the community was incorporated. The fall, 1975, issue of the *Communicator*, official quarterly government publication, announced that Wilmette's new administration building was scheduled to be completed and ready for occupancy by the end of November, and "will permit the Village to again have its major administrative offices under one roof." The Village Hall houses the Park District, which had been located in Laurel School, and provides offices for all Village

New Administration Building, Summer, 1976. Centennial Fountain is in the foreground. Photograph shows the park-like surroundings of the building, completed in 1975. Designed by Coder Taylor, the building took two years to complete, and has underground parking. (Courtesy Coder Taylor)

Dedication Ceremony, July 4, 1976. Assembled for formal ceremonies are many Village officials, past and present. Shown at the microphone is Village president Warren Burmeister, and to the right is former mayor James A. Schwietert. (Courtesy Milton Stern)

departments as well as council chambers. Murals of early Wilmette, removed from the 1910 Village Hall before demolition, and portraits of Archange Ouilmette and John D. Westerfield, painted in the thirties by the late George Lusk, a W.P.A. artist, have been newly framed for the new administration building.

Landscaping was completed by the following spring, and the long-planned Centennial Fountain was incorporated into the design for the front lawn of the building. The new facility was dedicated on July 4, 1976, with the participation of former trustees and village presidents and their successors in office, those who had planned the building, and those who implemented the plans.

In 1976, four years after celebrating Wilmette's Centennial, organizations and residents are observing the nation's Bicentennial. Taking a leading role during the first half of 1976 has been the Wilmette Bicentennial Commission under chairman Olene Sailor. Special events included the opening of the Bicentennial year with a Park District Wilmette Children's Theater production of *GEORGE M.!*, a winter concert of Civil War band music sponsored by the Wilmette Historical Society, and special historical exhibits from each of the community's churches. Northridge Woman's Club created a July historical costume exhibit for the shop windows at Plaza del Lago, and the school children and scout troops have had many special events. One light-hearted project was the painting of fireplugs across the Village, to resemble revolutionary soldiers. The publication of this book has been a major project of the Wilmette Bicentennial Commission, production responsibilities handled by Heritage Chairman John P. Ryan.

Our village has come a very long way since the time when this was a place of thick woods and a few scattered houses. But the physical evolution from forest to modern suburb has also been matched by a continuing determination to keep Wilmette a place in which we and our children are proud to live. The very heart of this community pride exists in the preservation of history. The village is fortunate to have received historical materials from those now deceased, as well as from those who by their sharing of these materials today, demonstrate their hope that Wilmette's history shall continue into future generations.

Appendix

VILLAGE PRESIDENTS OF WILMETTE

1872 — 1976

1872-1873	John Gedney Westerfield	1897-1898	George E. Fernald
1873-1874	Benjamin M. Munn	1898-1899	Louis J. Pierson
1874-1875	Andrew Taylor Sherman	1899-1900	Joseph Lyman McKittrick
1875-1878	Amos Shantz	1900-1902	George W. Springer
1878-1880	Hubbard Latham	1902-1906	Henry B. Gates
1880-1883	John W. Finney	1906-1915	John Dubois Couffer
1883-1886	Frank L. Joy*	1915-1917	Oscar Weber Schmidt
1886-1887	Rev. William Netstraeter*	1917-1925	Edward Zipf
1887-1888	Milton C. Springer*	1925-1931	Earl E. Orner
1888-1889	William Panushka	1931-1935	Carbon P. Dubbs
1889-1890	Frank L. Joy*	1935-1945	Harry Clark Kinne
1890-	Milton C. Springer* (Died in Office)	1945-1953	William H. Alexander
		1953-1957	William H. McKnight
1890-1891	Rev. William Netstraeter*	1957-1961	John C. Sanderson, Jr.
1891-1892	Frank L. Joy*	1961-1965	Howard C. Decker
1892-1893	Edgar T. Paul	1965-1969	Kenneth P. Santee
1893-1895	Samuel S. Dingee	1969-1973	James A. Schwietert
1895-1897	Horace Greeley Drury	1973-	Warren L. Burmeister

* indicates more than one term

The Big Tree. Photograph at left shows the tree around 1900, before it was reduced to a 30-foot stump. Closeup, right, shows the hollow entrance at the base.

TRAIL TREES AND BIG TREE

Where the white settlers relied on the Green Bay Trail and made paths and roads to reach their destinations, the Pottawatomie Indians of the Wilmette area used their own natural system to mark trails through the thick woods, to chipping stations where they hammered out arrowheads and stone implements, and to their villages. A hardwood sapling growing close to the trail was selected, and the tip bent so the tiny trunk was parallel to the ground. The tip was usually tied down with vines, or sometimes buried in the ground, pointing along the trail to be followed. The tree tip would soon die, and a new growth would begin upward. The trail tree was therefore a living marker, which would live as long as the tree itself. Trail trees were often spaced from 500 to 1,000 feet apart.

Of many trail trees in what is now Wilmette, only two authenticated trail trees remain. One is located in front of the house on the northeast corner of Greenwood and Tenth Street, on the parkway, and bends to the northeast, marking the trail to the lake. The other tree is in the front yard of the house at 17 Canterbury Court. Both trees are marked with permanent plaques, authenticating their use. These trees, probably well over 200 years old, are America's first road signs.

In the early 1900's, a huge cottonwood tree stood on the farm then owned by the Kloepfer family on Glenview Road west of Skokie Boulevard. The tree was more than 160 feet high, and there was an opening more than eight feet high in the base, leading to a large hollow space inside 20 feet high. Pottawatomie Indians were said to have used the hollow tree for council meetings and dances. After fire and lightning destroyed much of the old tree, according to a recent item in the Beeline column of the *Chicago Daily News*, it was purchased about 1903 and moved to the present site of Dyche Stadium parking lot by Richard Gloede, owner of a horticulture business. Estimated as more than 600 years old, the remaining stump was destroyed when the stadium lot was built in the early 1950's. Black Hawk, the Sauk chief, was also said to have used it as a place of council during the Black Hawk War in 1832.

1890 Wilmette Village Hall.
Outgrown by 1910, the
building was purchased and
moved to Park Avenue, and
is presently in use as a
private residence.

Wilmette Street Names Have Changed

Present Name	Former Name	Derivation of Original Name
Ashland ave.	Fifth ave.	Counting from Central avenue
Beechwood ave.	Kenilworth Dr. N.	Extension of a Kenilworth street
Birchwood ave.	Seger st.	for Joseph Seger, developer
Blackhawk road[1]	Liberty st.	
Catalpa place	Doyle court	For early settler
Central ave.[2]	George st.	For George McDaniel
Central Park ave.	Nanzig ave.	For Paul Nanzig
Chestnut ave.	Sixth ave.[3]	Counting from Central avenue
Colgate st.	Forest ave.	
Cornell st.	Oxford st.	
Dartmouth st.	Alles st.	For Alles family
Elmwood ave.	North ave.	North reservation boundary
Green Bay rd.	W. Railroad ave.[4]	
Greenleaf ave.	Depot Pl.	C. & N. W. Ry. Station
Greenwood ave.	Fourth ave.[5]	Counting from Central avenue
Greenwood ave.[6]	Franz st.	
Harvard st.	Brown st.	
Illinois road	Happ rd.[7]	For Happ family
Iroquois rd.[1]	Union st.	
Keating ave.	Kilpatrick ave.	
Kenilworth ave.	Kenilworth dr. S.	Extension of a Kenilworth street
Knox ave.	Maple ave.	
Laurel ave.	Michigan st.[8]	
Lawndale st.	Eighteenth st.	
Linden ave.[2]	James st.	For James Kline
Lockerbie lane	Lowler ave.[9]	
Maple ave.	Hill st.	For B. F. Hill
Michigan ave.	Sheridan ave.	
Oak Circle	Horse Shoe Curve	
Oakwood ave.	South ave.	South limits of village
Park ave.	West ave.	West limit of First Subdivision
Prairie ave.	Kline st.	For Simon Veeder Kline
Ramona rd.	Miami rd.[10]	
Sheridan Rd.	Central ave.[11]	
Thornwood ave.	Barklay ave.	
Walnut ave.	Greenwood ave.[12]	
Washington ave.[2]	Charles st.	For Charles Westerfield[13]
Washington ave.[14]	Blum st.	For Lambert Blum
Wilmette ave.[15]	Gross Point rd.	Gross Point to Ridgeville
Wood court	Greenwood st.	
Second st.[16]	Fifth st.	Counting from present 7th st.
Third st.	Fourth st.	Counting from present 7th st.
Fourth st.	Third st.[17]	Counting from present 7th st.
Fifth st.	Second st.	Counting from present 7th st.
Sixth st.	First st.	Counting from present 7th st.
Seventh st.	Grove st.	
Eighth st.	Division st.	East edge of first plat
Ninth st.	Henry st.	For Henry Dingee
Tenth st.	Alexander st.[18]	For Alexander McDaniel
Eleventh st.[19]	John st.	For John G. Westerfield
Eleventh st.[20]	William st.	For William H. Kinney
Twelfth st.	Park st.	
Thirteenth st.[21]	Gage st.	For Gage family
Thirteenth st.[2]	Bennett st.	Extension of an Evanston street
Fourteenth st.	Foster st.	
Fifteenth st.	Elm st.	
Sixteenth st.	Oak st.	
Seventeenth st.	Walnut st.[22]	
Eighteenth st.	Fernleaf st.[23]	
Twentieth st.	Cambridge st.[24]	
Twenty-First st.	Melvin st.[25]	
Twenty-Second st.	Princeton st.	
Twenty-Third st.	Greeley ave.	
Twenty-Fourth st.	Wentworth ave.	
Twenty-Fifth st.	Hancock st.	
Twenty-Sixth st.	Sherman st.	
Poplar Drive	East Railroad avenue	

Although Lake, Central, Linden, and Wilmette Avenues retain their original names, much else has changed. Division street, the former east edge of the village, is now Eighth street. Some streets were named for the early settlers and promoters. Henry Street (now Ninth) was named for Henry Dingee; Alexander street (now Tenth) for Alexander McDaniel; John street (now the south part of Eleventh) for John Westerfield, the first village president; James Street (now the western end of Linden Avenue) for James Kline; and Charles street (now Washington avenue), for Charles Westerfield or Charles Vail, both of whom served as village clerk in the early days.

The old west line of the village is now Fifteenth street. What was once Gross Point Road is now parts of Wilmette and Prairie Avenues. West street is now Park Avenue. George street is now part of Central Avenue; old Park street is now Twelfth street; and Gage street, named for that prominent family, is now Thirteenth street.

Depot place was later extended and became Greenleaf avenue. South avenue is now Oakwood avenue.

West Railroad avenue later became Main street, and still more recently Green Bay road. The last name was chosen to conform with the name used by Evanston, Kenilworth and Winnetka. It does not follow the old Green Bay trail.

FOOTNOTES
1. west of Romona road
2. west of railroad
3. also Clover avenue
4. also Main street
5. also Hollywood avenue
6. west of 23rd St.
7. also Avoca road, Reinwald avenue, Ashland avenue
8. also Bryan street
9. also Summers street
10. also Spruce street
11. also Grove street, 7th st., and State street
12. also Columbus street
13. or Charles Gedney, Charles Kline, or Charles Vail
14. west of the ridge
15. west of Kline street (Prairie)
16. vacated—occupied by the North Shore channel
17. also Meridian street
18. part of Wilmette avenue north of Elmwood
19. south of Lake avenue
20. north of Lake avenue
21. east of railroad
22. south of Wilmette avenue called Hoefer street
23. also Maple street
24. also Clark street
25. also Oak street and Pine street

The following streets have apparently retained their original names: Broadway, Central(21), Forest, Lake, Linden (21), Washington (21), Woodbine avenue, and Isabella street.

1894 Gross Point Village Hall, Circa 1965. The large brick building on Ridge Road served as Police Dept., Fire Dept., jail, and Village Trustee meetings were held on the first floor. The second floor, a large undivided room 35x60, was used for community dances and parties. Presently occupied by the Wilmette Newspaper Distributors, the front of the building has been altered, a second floor balcony removed; inside, much of the building remains as it was in 1894.

The Hotel That Was Never Built. The engraving represented here is the plan for the Wilmette Hotel, which was to have been erected in the spring of 1875. It was to have been one of the best hotels in the vicinity of Chicago and cost $20,000. Construction was to have been of wood, three stories high with a basement and a Mansard roof.

WILMETTE HOTEL.

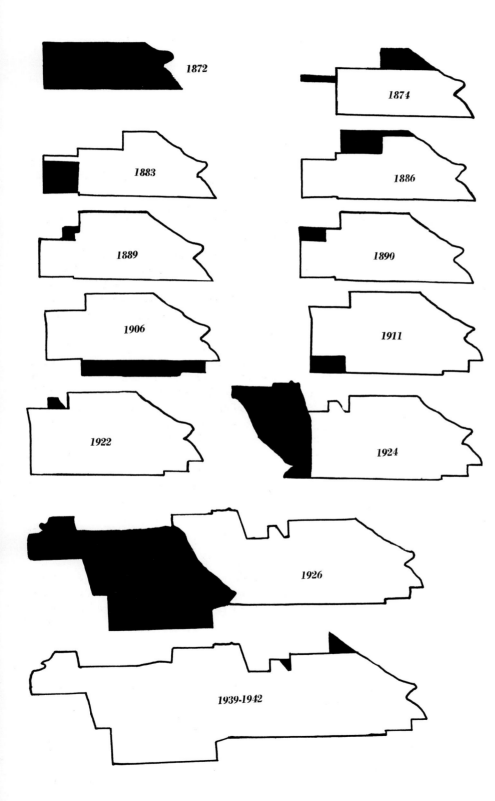

Expansion of Wilmette
is tracing in the outline
maps at left. As incorporated
in 1872 the Village occupied
the northern part of the old
Ouilmette land grant. Text
at right explains details of
each annexation. (Outline
maps originally published
in the *Wilmette Life*,
September, 1947.)

1872: In the beginning, the boundaries were Lake Michigan and (using the present names), Elmwood Avenue, Fifteenth Street, and the line of Oakwood Avenue.

1874: Expansion began. Two areas were added: 1/Milton Wilson's addition in the northeast was bounded by 10th Street, Elmwood Avenue, Chestnut Avenue, and the lake; 2/B. M. Munn (Village president that year) and Palmer's addition, a one block strip (between Lake and Forest Avenues) from 15th Street to Ridge Road. Thus in one year, Wilmette grew beyond the north and west boundaries of the old reservation.

In that year, too, Wilmette gained an immediate neighbor, for west of Ridge Road the Village of Gross Point was incorporated. Still to the north and south were stretches of unincorporated land.

1883: The tract bounded by Lake Avenue, 15th Street, Wilmette Avenue, and Ridge Road was annexed.

1886: This was the year the Gage additon was made to the Village. This was an irregular area, extending from Elmwood Avenue near the C&NW RR tracks east to 10th Street and north a half-block beyond Chestnut Avenue, plus an additional area north of Chestnut Avenue all the way to the lake.

1889: This addition, and the one the following year, were subdivisions developed by Edgar T. Paul, real estate man and one-time Village president. This was an "L" shaped tract north of Forest Avenue between 15th and 16th Streets, plus a "corridor" north of Elmwood Avenue as far east as the Gage addition.

1890: Mr. Paul was also responsible for the boundary expansion the following year. This tract extended from 16th Street west to the Gross Point line at Ridge Road and from Forest Avenue north to a line a half-block north of Elmwood Avenue.

In 1896, the Village of Kenilworth was incorporated and the two communities met at the point where Chestnut Avenue bends to become Cumnor Road.

1906: In this year, Wilmette expanded to the south to meet Evanston at Isabella Street. The new addition extended west to 15th Street, the old west line of the Indian land grant, and east to Sheridan Road. East of Sheridan Road, north as far as the line of Oakwood Avenue, was Evanston, and Evanston, too, got a tract a half-block deep north of Isabella Street between Third Street and Sheridan Road. The eastern part of this annexation had been variously known as Hillville and as Llewellyn Park.

1911: The expansion to the south was completed when the rectangle bounded by Isabella Street, Ridge Road, Wilmette Avenue, and 15th Street was added to the Village of Wilmette.

1922: The building boom which followed the First World War made land values soar. The area shown in the map for 1922, bounded by the C&NW RR tracks, Glendenning Road, Ashland Avenue, and the old north limits, was once golf course and marsh. The rest of the area between the tracks and Ridge Road went to Kenilworth.

1924: The Village of Gross Point was dissolved and much of the former territory was voted into Wilmette; Illinois Road became the new west line of Wilmette. Parts of old Gross Point went to Evanston, Kenilworth, and Winnetka, and some of it, around the Indian Hill Golf club is still unincorporated.

1926: The North Shore electric line was building its Skokie valley route and Wilmette pushed its limits west once more. North of Lake Avenue it reached the east fork of the north branch of the Chicago River; south of Lake Avenue, it stopped just short of the tracks. So that year, Wilmette touched borders with two additional communities, Glenview and Skokie (then Niles Center).

1939: A small unincorporated triangle, just to the east of the tracks between Kenilworth and Wilmette became "Connecticut Village" and was annexed to Wilmette. 1942:

1942: Another "orphan" between Kenilworth and Wilmette was No Man's Land, along the lake shore. Part commercial, part residential, sometimes part honky-tonk, it had been a problem to both Wilmette and Kenilworth for years. After a generation of effort, Wilmette annexed the section.

Note: In the sketch maps at left, the lake shore is shown as it is in 1976. The harbor silhouette is made land, most of Gillson Park having been under water back in 1872.

BIBLIOGRAPHY

BOOKS, BOOKLETS and PAMPHLETS

"Antoine Ouilmette," Frank R. Grover. 1908: Evanston Historical Society. Evanston: Bowman Publishing Company.

"Dingee Family Record,", Annie W. Dingee. No date. Wilmette Historical Museum.

"Evanston — Its Land and Its People," Viola Crouch Reeling. 1928: Fort Dearborn Chapter, Daughters of the American Revolution.

"Frontiers of Old Wilmette," Herbert B. Mulford, May 1953. Collection of articles written for the *Wilmette Life*, 1952 and 1953.

"Know Your Town — Wilmette, Illinois," League of Women Voters of Wilmette, April, 1939.

"Little Journeys to Historical Wilmette," Herbert B. Mulford. No date, but known to be prior to 1955. Wilmette Public Library.

"Spotlight on Wilmette: 1956," League of Women Voters of Wilmette, November, 1956.

"Story of Wilmette," Herbert B. Mulford. 1950: Wilmette Public Schools.

"Wilmette and the Suburban Whirl," Herbert B. Mulford, 1956.

Plan of Wilmette — The Report of the Wilmette Plan Commission, 1922. Wilmette Plan Commission. Press of James Watson & Company, Chicago.

Wilmette Directory — 1898. Wilmette Printing Company, Wilmette.

NEWSPAPERS, MAGAZINES, SPECIAL SOURCES

"Along the North Shore," undated paper in Wilmette Public Library files, no author.

"Beeline," Item about the Indian council tree in west Wilmette, *Chicago Daily News*, April 10, 1976.

"A Brief History of the Wilmette Public Schools . . .," research paper by Millard D. Bell, superintendent of Wilmette schools, 1942-1965. 1965.

"Early Chicagoland," Philip Hanson. *Field Museum of Natural History Bulletin, May, 1976.*

"Hoffman Letters." Collection in typed manuscript form. Private Collection.

"Ouilmette Settles Village," *Chicago Tribune*, August 24, 1972.

"Wilmette, Home of Chicago's First 'Commuter'," *Bell Telephone News,* September, 1925.

Wilmette Life Centennial Supplement, April 27, 1972.

"Wilmette — The Second Century" Special edition, April 24, 1973.

Microfilms — October, 1925-December, 1975, various dates.

Woman's Club Bulletin, March, 1931. 40th Anniversary Issue, Woman's Club of Wilmette.

Extensive materials and illustrations from the files of the Wilmette Public Library and the Wilmette Historical Museum.

Index

LOOKING TO THE FUTURE...

All of those who have worked on this book, like those who have worked on historical materials in the ten decades past, hope to minimize error, be factual, yet make history interesting, and deal as fully with the subject as space will allow. We hope that you will be interested in contributing to the future, and will help to supplement present information by correcting our information where you believe you can provide more accurate and complete details.

There are many phases of Village history which could, by themselves, occupy an entire book. As a result, some events or periods may have been treated in less depth than they might have been if we had more space. On the other hand, there are areas where we have little or no information, and were limited by it. If you have materials that you feel would be of interest to others, would you send it along to us?

We would like to know:

1/ the dates, places and people involved;
2/ how you came to know if it (from another person, letters, newspaper, etc.)
3/ whether you have any letters, documents, clippings or photographs which would be pertinent to the event or story.

We have some funds available to copy photographs and documents, so that the owner would not be required to donate the original if he wished to keep it.

Please write to The Wilmette Historical Society, P.O. Box 96, Wilmette, Illinois 60091. Please do not send original manuscripts or pictures until we request them—if you can, send a xerox copy so we may see what the material is—that will reduce the risk of loss. We welcome photographs, documents and artifacts relating to the history of Wilmette, and hope that you will share them with the community, for future generations.